GOD IN MY CORNER

BY GEORGE FOREMAN
WITH KEN ABRAHAM

THOMAS NELSON
Since 1798

NASHVILLE   DALLAS   MEXICO CITY   RIO DE JANEIRO

Published in Nashville, Tennessee, by Thomas Nelson. Thomas Nelson is a registerred trademark of Thomas Nelson, Inc.

Thomas Nelson, Inc. books may be purchased in bulk for educational, business, fund-raising, or sales promotional use. For information, please e-mail SpecialMarkets@ThomasNelson.com.

All Scripture quotations, unless otherwise indicated, are taken from the New King James Version®. Copyright © 1982 by Thomas Nelson, Inc. Used by permission. All rights reserved.

Other Scripture references are from the New American Standard Bible (NASB), © 1960, 1977 by the Lockman Foundation.

Editorial Staff: Greg Daniel, acquisition editor, and Thom Chittom, managing editor
Cover Design: Designworks
Page Design: Casey Hooper

Published in association with the literary agency of Mark Sweeney & Associates,

ISBN: 978-1-4003-398-5 (TP)

Library of Congress Cataloging-in-Publication Data
Foreman, George, 1949-
  God in my corner / by George Foreman with Ken Abraham.
    p. cm.
  Includes bibliographical references and index.
    ISBN 10: 0-8499-0314-9 (hardcover)
    ISBN 13: 978-0-8499-0314-4 (hardcover)
    ISBN 10: 0-8499-1908-8 (IE)
    ISBN 13: 978-0-8499-1908-4 (IE)
  1. Foreman, George, 1949- 2. Christian biography--United States. 3.
Christian life. I. Abraham, Ken. II. Title.
  BR1725.F547A3 2007
  277.3'082092--dc22
  [B]
                                                                    2007006016

CONTENTS

1
THE PHONE CALL THAT CHANGED MY LIFE

Everyone needs a second chance, even if your name is George Foreman. You might know me as the guy on television who advertises the George Foreman grills, Meineke Car Care, or Casual Male Big & Tall clothes. If you follow sports, you may know me as the world's heavyweight boxing champion who lost to Muhammad Ali and then came back twenty years later to win the heavyweight title again at forty-five years of age.

But what few people know is that something incredibly strange happened to me on the evening of March 17, 1977. That supernatural experience defined my life so dramatically that it divided my identity into two Georges. The old George lived prior to that day, which I'll refer to as "my first time around." Ever since then, I've been the new George. God gave me another chance at life, and I've been determined to do it right this time.

When we start out in life, we often travel down some wrong roads, hurting ourselves and others along the way. Most of us have to hit bottom before the lightbulb turns on and we realize that we've blown it. It's at that critical moment that we must seize the opportunity and change directions. We must start traveling down a different road, leading to a new destination.

My second chance arrived unexpectedly in a Puerto Rican dressing room after a heavyweight boxing match. What happened to me in that room is so incredibly bizarre, it's unlikely you've ever before read anything like it. Simply stated, *I died and went to the other side.* The experience impacted me so profoundly that three decades later I can't go a single day without thinking about it.

THE CRISIS I COULDN'T FIX

December 1976. The phone rang in the middle of the night, rousing me out of a deep sleep. Through foggy eyes, I strained to read the clock on my nightstand.

It's nearly three o'clock in the morning. Who in the world is calling me at this hour? Don't they know that no one is supposed to disturb me when I'm preparing for a fight?

In three months, I was scheduled to fight Jimmy Young in a highly touted heavyweight boxing match in San Juan, Puerto Rico. I had been training vigorously on my ranch in Marshall, Texas, and everyone on my training team and household staff knew the rules: No one was supposed to distract me while I was in training. The word around camp was: "Don't bother George. If something good happens, it can wait. If something bad happens, keep quiet about it around George. If someone dies, don't tell him."

A boxer has to stay in the right frame of mind to prepare well. Boxing isn't just about the grueling physical training—running mile after mile, hitting the punching bags thousands of times, and sparring round after round. A huge part of boxing is mental preparation. If you lose the bout inside your mind, you'll lose it in the ring, too. That's why orders were given to not interrupt me for *any* reason. But whoever was calling at this late hour obviously chose to disregard the training rules.

My mother had come to my training camp to cook for me, and was sleeping in my bedroom while I slept in another room in the back of the house. Apparently, the ringing telephone woke Mom up as well. Rubbing my eyes trying to fully wake up, I picked up the phone at the same time my mother did in her bedroom.

I recognized my sister, Mary, crying on the other end of the line. It shook Mom when she heard her sobs. "What's wrong, Mary?" she asked, worry clearly evident in her voice.

Mary composed herself well enough to reply. "My son was playing outside and had a seizure," she said. "By the time we got him to the doctor, he was in a coma. The doctors don't think he's going to make it. They say if he does come out of the coma, he won't be able to walk or talk." Mary broke down in violent sobs again.

The boy she was talking about was my five-year-old nephew, George Edward Dumas. Little George was one of my family's favorites; he touched a soft spot in my heart, and he looked up to me like a father. Although I was deeply concerned about George's condition, I didn't want to hear another word. I knew I had to stay in my "zone" and stay focused on training.

I quietly hung up the phone, pretending the conversation never took place. As I lay in bed with my head on my pillow, my eyes wide open and staring at the ceiling, I thought, *I didn't hear that. This can't be happening. I have to stay focused.*

No way. As soon as I heard my mother hang up, I jumped out of bed and ran to her bedroom. "Momma, you tell those doctors I'm George Foreman, the boy's uncle. You tell them whatever it costs, I'll pay for it. Tell them to fly in the best doctors, and I'll take care of the bills. You tell them who I am."

"Son," she explained, "they already have the best doctors."

I wouldn't take no for an answer. "Mom, you pick up that phone and call them right now. You tell them that I'm George Foreman, and I'll take care of everything!"

"Okay, George. I'll try."

I marched back to my bedroom carrying a huge load of worry. I nervously tossed and turned, realizing my nephew would probably die. If he survived, he would never be normal. I mulled the situation over in my mind. *That boy didn't bother anyone. He's in a coma and can't wake up.*

If he does awaken, he's going to be paralyzed and will never be able to speak or walk again.

Unable to sleep, I couldn't rest until I knew what the doctors had to say. I threw back the sheets and stomped back down the hallway. "Momma, did you call them?"

"Yes, I called and told them. Son, you're just going to have to pray."

In stunned disbelief, I slowly trudged back to my room. When someone tells you the only thing you can do is pray, *that's bad.*

Then it hit me: *All of George Foreman's money can't resolve this crisis.* All of my fame, fortune, and friends couldn't fix this problem. I was powerless to do anything to help. That little boy's future was out of my hands, and the doctors' hands, too. They had done the best they could, but sometimes the best human efforts aren't enough.

That's when a lot of people turn to prayer. When humans can't fix a problem, they'll cry out for divine assistance. If there's a God, maybe He can help. For somebody like me, prayer was a last resort. I had never really prayed before, simply because I didn't need to. I didn't believe in all that religious stuff, anyhow. My money always fixed all of my problems.

I didn't need God. I was George Foreman, Olympic gold medalist and heavyweight champion of the world. I had tasted the best this world has to offer, but I had also experienced the worst, growing up in a poor section of Houston.

ALWAYS HUNGRY

I knew firsthand what it was like to live in poverty. My alcoholic father, J. D. Foreman, worked on the railroad and didn't live at home most of the time, leaving my mom to provide for her seven children. Her salary of $26 per week didn't stretch far when eight mouths wanted food. I was a big boy, so I was *always* hungry. It wasn't till years later, after I started boxing, that I could remember my stomach feeling full after a meal.

Mom sometimes brought home a single hamburger for her kids and herself to divide. It was such a luxury; I grew up believing hamburgers were only for rich people. She would tear it into eight pieces, and we all got one bite. I savored the few seconds it stayed in my mouth, dreaming of the day when

I might get to eat an entire hamburger by myself. Every other Sunday, she made us pancakes and allotted one small piece of bacon to each child.

Breakfast usually consisted of a bowl of cornflakes covered with watered-down milk. Hardly the breakfast of champions. School lunches weren't any better. Most of the time I carried a mayonnaise sandwich to school with me. Every now and then, my mother would slip in a thin piece of luncheon meat. I drank water with it, wishing I could afford one of those little cartons of milk that cost six cents.

Sometimes, when I was playing with the neighborhood kids, their parents would call them home to eat lunch. I had no lunch waiting for me, so I would peek through the windows and watch my friends eat. My mouth watered as I'd see them tear the crust off their bread. Then they'd pull the chicken skins off their drumsticks because they didn't want them. I thought, *I would love to eat what they don't want.* I wished they would have asked me to take their scraps out to the dogs so I could get a bite to eat too.

My mother, Nancy Ree Foreman, had grown up in poverty, being the daughter of a sharecropper who made his eight children work for him. Although she was intelligent and desperately wanted an education, she never had the opportunity to pursue it. Her father continually made her promises he didn't keep. "Just help me out this year, and you can go to school next year." But "next year" never came, and my mother never received the education she so sincerely desired.

> I WISHED THEY WOULD HAVE ASKED ME TO TAKE THEIR SCRAPS OUT TO THE DOGS SO I COULD GET A BITE TO EAT TOO.

When I was still a little boy, my mother became very sick; she was coughing constantly, wheezing, and generally feeling awful for prolonged periods of time. When she finally consented to seek medical attention, the doctor told her that she had contracted tuberculosis and needed to go to the hospital right away. My mother thought it would be a short stay, but as it turned out, she had to remain in the hospital for more than a year!

During that time, I was pretty much on my own, so I spent most of my days and nights out on the streets, getting into trouble.

In my early years, my mother was the only one who could control me.

My dad wasn't around much as I was growing up, since he and Mom had broken up their marriage. My mother was tall and slender—not a large woman at all—but she was strong, and she believed in that adage, "Spare the rod, spoil the child." Usually, my mother didn't take time to find a rod when it came to disciplining me; she'd reach for whatever was close by—a belt, a big shoe, or whatever she could find—and she'd clobber me with it. Mom could throw a powerful punch too! And she wasn't above using a judo chop or a swift kick to "motivate" me or correct me when I did wrong.

But with my mother fighting tuberculosis in the hospital, I ran wild, constantly getting into fights out on the streets. Yet somehow, even with her diminished stamina, my mother heard about my unsavory activities and contacted someone from social services. She told them, "I'm here in the hospital, and I know my children are having some problems at home. But I could rest well if they would just watch this one boy of mine." My mother had seven children, but you can guess which child she was most concerned about.

The social services representative contacted a wonderful woman by the name of Bonner to help look after me. Ms. Bonner lived way out of town, but she came into the city looking for me, hoping to spend some time with me. She took an interest in me and tried to help me stay out of trouble while my mom was in the hospital. One day Ms. Bonner told me, "George, I'm going to come over on the weekend, and I'd like you to come back home with me to cut my grass. I'll pay you for working."

"Can I have a couple of my friends come along, too?" I asked.

"Sure you can," Ms. Bonner answered.

That weekend, Ms. Bonner picked up two of my friends and me and drove us out of town to her place. She took us to the shed and showed us the lawn mower. "Okay, George, you can mow the grass. You other fellows can do the trim and follow behind him to rake up the cuttings."

"Well, Ms. Bonner, my buddy here," I said, pointing to one of my friends, "his dad has a lawn mower. He knows how to do it better than I would. Maybe I should let him mow the grass."

"No, George," she said, "I want *you* to do it."

"Really?"

"That's right. You are in charge, George."

"But his dad has a . . ."

"You!"

I looked at Ms. Bonner, then at my buddies. I said, "Okay, guys; let's get going." We worked at Ms. Bonner's all day long, and I felt so good when she handed me some money as payment. More importantly, I felt good about myself.

I didn't realize it fully at the time, but looking back on that experience, I now understand that Ms. Bonner was allowing me to be *somebody*. For the first time in my life, a non-family member was telling me, "You can do it, George. I believe in you!"

To this day, my life is indebted to Ms. Bonner. That little dash of self-esteem she helped to foster in me is still with me today. Ms. Bonner made me feel so good about myself, and part of the reason I am who I am today is because of Ms. Bonner.

Ms. Bonner stayed in touch with me until my mom was discharged. Unfortunately, when my mother got out of the hospital, I went right back to my old ways of stealing and beating up people.

Mom didn't have time to attend church when I was a boy—she was always working, trying to earn enough to keep us alive—but she recognized the value of church, and she believed we'd be better kids if we could get enough Bible in us. Every so often, she'd thrust a Bible in my direction and say, "Here, George. You need to get in that room and read this Bible."

I'd take the Bible, flip through the pages and look at the pictures for a while, and then return the Book to my mother.

"See there. Don't you feel better now?" she'd ask hopefully.

"Oh yeah, Mom. I feel a lot better now," I lied.

By the time I was sixteen years of age, I was a vicious, savage teenager, picking fights in school or wherever I went. Not surprisingly, I dropped out of school in ninth grade and started looking for a job. But not too many people want to hire a ninth-grade dropout. Eventually, I took a job washing dishes in a restaurant.

I figured that my only way out of poverty was to use my fists and fight my way out. Sometimes I beat up two or three people a day. I was brutal, too. One time I walked up to a guy who hadn't done anything to me, and without warning, I punched him right in the face, just to be nasty. He hit the dirt like a rock. I walked away with him still laid out semi-conscious on the ground. Because my conscience was so encrusted with hate, it didn't bother me to see people bleeding or knocked out cold. Many times, I mugged people just to get some drinking money. I was really good at beating up people, although it never dawned on me at the time that one day people would pay to watch me fight.

My older brother Robert—we called him Sonny; his friends called him "Rags"—was a hardworking family man with a wife and two children. Ten years older than me, Sonny lived in a nice house and earned a good living by working for a moving company, Wald Transfer and Storage. Sonny recognized that I was heading in the wrong direction, so he offered to help me get a job with Wald.

"It's hard work," Sonny told me, "but if you do a good job and the bosses like you, they may put you on full time, and you can be a regular." I really wanted to be a "regular," too, since if my boss hired me full time, the company provided a uniform with my name embroidered above the pocket.

I went to work for Wald and quickly discovered that my brother was telling me the truth—it was hard work, with long, grueling hours, often from eight in the morning till midnight, but I earned $1.25 per hour for loading and unloading heavy furniture. That was more money than I could count! Wald specialized in "office moves," moving the file cabinets, desks, business machines, and other heavy items from one office building to another. The items were big, bulky, and heavy, but I was young and strong, so when I saw my bosses watching, I'd give it all the extra "oomph" I could muster. Before long, I'd made a good impression on them as well as my co-workers. After work, my new friends helped me spend a good portion of my earnings on alcohol. What was left, I used to help my mom.

One day, the boss informed our crew that we had a high-priority office move that we needed to get done quickly. We'd have to work from early in the morning till midnight every day until we could get it all done. The first day was bad enough, with all that heavy lifting and carrying. After the second day, I was dead tired, my back was sore, and I was ready to quit. By the end of the third day, I was exhausted. When we took our dinner break around five o'clock in the afternoon, the boss instructed us to be back in an hour. I was so worn out, I went home and fell asleep. I didn't wake up until the following morning.

I was so ashamed of myself, I never went back to work at Wald, not even to pick up my paycheck. I knew that I had not only disobeyed my boss, and probably forfeited any chance of getting the uniform with my name on it, but I'd also embarrassed my brother, Sonny. The other guys on the crew teased him incessantly. "Rags' brother couldn't carry the load. Rags' brother took a break for dinner, and old Rags' lazy brother never came back."

"Where were you? Why didn't you come back?" Sonny asked me when I talked to him about my disappearing act.

"Man, I was just too tired," I told him honestly.

The following week, Sonny and I talked again, and he told me that Wald had some big moves coming up, and they needed to hire some extra help. Sonny thought they might be willing to hire me if I went and told the boss the truth. "You're strong and you're a hard worker," Sonny said to me. "The bosses like that. Just tell the boss that you have an explanation why you didn't come back," Sonny suggested, "and I think he'll not only take you back, but he will hire you full time. Just apologize and make up a good explanation."

I wasn't quite sure what an "explanation" was—it wasn't a word I used. But I figured it was worth a try if I could get my job back.

I went to see the moving company crew chief, a tough guy who had been moving furniture for longer than I had been alive. "I'd like to get my job back," I told him. When the boss saw me, he didn't even want to look at me, much less carry on a conversation about rehiring me. "You walked off the job, Foreman," he said curtly.

"I know; yes, I did, sir. But I have an es . . . ex . . ." My mind was drawing a blank. *What was that word Sonny told me to use?* "I have an esclanation!" I finally blurted.

The boss glared at me as he threw my pay envelope in my direction. "Look, Foreman; I don't want to hear about your *esclanation*! Take your money and get out of here. Don't you ever come back around here no more. If I see you around here, I'm going to call the cops."

"But, but . . ."

"Take your money and your esclanation and hit the road."

LEARNING TO BOX

Out of school and out of work, I scrambled for any odd jobs to make a few measly dollars. About that time, my sister Mary told me about the Job Corps, a skill-learning program that was part of President Lyndon Johnson's "War on Poverty." I decided to apply for the Job Corps in the hope of learning a skill so I could earn a living. I had seen the famous Baltimore Colts quarterback Johnny Unitus as well as All-Pro, Cleveland Browns running back Jim Brown, on TV public-service ads inviting people like me to join. Jim Brown was my childhood hero, pointing me in the direction I needed to go. I thought sure Jim would be proud of me for joining, so I signed up.

The Job Corps Training Center was located in Grants Pass, Oregon, a long way from Houston, in every sense of the word. At the Job Corps, I met people who cared about me and believed in me. They provided three meals a day, and the instructors taught me how to use a hammer correctly as well as other practical skills. But even at the Job Corps, I continued my mean, bullying ways, getting in fights and cold-cocking anyone who looked at me crossways. One night, some guys and I were listening to the Cassius Clay–Floyd Patterson fight on the radio when one of the guys that I had beaten up challenged me, "Hey, George. If you're so tough, why don't you become a boxer?"

"All right, I will," I retorted. "I'll show you." Few if any of the guys in that room took me seriously, including me. But I'd said it, and I couldn't back down.

After six months in Oregon, I was transferred to another Job Corps center near Pleasanton, California, where I was to receive more focused vocational training. It was there that I met another man who would have a profound effect on my life.

I first saw Charles Broadus while I was standing in line my first day at the Pleasanton center. A stocky, muscular man, "Doc," as everyone called him, was head of security for the center. He was also in charge of the facility's sports activities.

I walked up to him, introduced myself, and said, "I want to be a boxer. Do you think I can?"

Doc Broadus looked me up and down and said, "You're big enough."

He paused and looked at me some more. "And you're ugly enough. Come on down to the gym."

Doc became a mentor to me. He taught me the difference between mere fighting and boxing. He told me, "If you will stay out of trouble, you can be a champion; you can win an Olympic gold medal."

Doc genuinely cared about me and treated me as a son. He had a lot of other young men to look after, many of whom were much better athletes than I was, but for some reason, Doc Broadus believed in me, and he helped me to believe in myself. Thanks to Doc, I felt that I could actually accomplish something in my life.

It was through the Job Corps that I first learned how to box. I knew how to hit people with my fists growing up in a tough neighborhood, but boxing was a whole new game. Although I had size and skills, I didn't know how to correctly throw punches and defend myself.

Doc had to start with me from scratch. I knew how to beat up on somebody, but boxing required more than just being able to bludgeon an opponent into submission. "If you want to be a boxer," Doc taught me, "you have to learn to box, not just fight." For one of my first bouts, he pointed to a skinny, young man and said, "I'm going to put you in the ring with him."

I didn't know whether to laugh or be insulted. I knew I could break that boy in half if I got ahold of him. Doc knew that I was unlikely to get ahold of him.

Excited about my first match, I went back to the dorm and told all the guys, "I'm going to be a boxer! Come on down to the gym and watch me." Several of them did. I was later glad that only a few showed up.

When Doc put me in the ring with the skinny guy, I figured that I would chew him up in a matter of seconds. I went after him with a vengeance, throwing punches in every direction, assuming I'd knock the boy out with one punch. Maybe I would have, if any of my punches would have landed.

But the boy knew something I didn't—he knew how to box, not just fight. He kept circling around me, bobbing and weaving, hitting me hard but never allowing himself to be hit.

Becoming more and more frustrated, I lunged at the boy, throwing a punch with all my might . . . and hit nothing but air. My momentum, however, carried me forward, and being totally off balance, I fell awkwardly to the mat. Again and again I went after him, with much the same results. The guys around the ring were laughing hilariously, some of them holding their sides from laughing so much. When it was all over, Doc didn't say anything. He just let the lesson sink in. I left the gym quickly and didn't go back. I'd been embarrassed enough and now had to fight even more ferociously in the dorm to silence the guys who had witnessed the skinny kid beat the daylights out of the Job Corps bully.

A few days later, I saw Doc Broadus on campus. "Where have you been?" he asked. "Why haven't you been down to the gym? Are you scared?"

"Me? Scared? No way. I . . . I . . . ah, er . . . I don't have any boxing shoes." Both Doc and I knew that I was merely making up an excuse, so Doc called my bluff.

"Sit down on the curb right there and wait. I need to go over to the office." He was only gone a few minutes when he returned from his office carrying a box containing a brand-new pair of boxing shoes. "I'll see you at the gym," he said.

With Doc's help, I started training hard, learning how to "bob and weave." As I gained experience, I fought in the Diamond Belt competition sponsored by the Job Corps, and I won a bunch of trophies. Next, I entered the Golden Gloves competition and won quite a few matches at that level, before finally losing at the national Golden Gloves tournament in Milwaukee. I was disappointed over this loss in particular because I slipped on the mat and the referee ruled it a "knockdown," but I didn't take it too hard. After all, I was about to graduate from the Job Corps and head back to Houston. While in the Job Corps, I had learned quite a bit about electronics, and I hoped to put my newfound skills to work. I planned to get an electronics-assembly job so I could help take better care of my mother.

When I graduated from the Job Corps in 1967, Doc Broadus appealed to me, almost begging me to consider other boxing options. "If you want to turn professional," he said, "I have a group of friends who will help sponsor you financially. If you want to work toward the Olympics, I'll help you do that." Doc believed in me, I knew, and maybe he recognized the potential danger of returning to my old stomping grounds.

I thanked Doc but turned him down and headed for home. My mother welcomed me back, and I set about filling out job applications. But even with my new skills, jobs didn't come quickly. I wasn't back in Houston for long before I started drinking and fighting again and slipping into some of my old patterns. Even my mother recognized that I needed a fresh start in a new environment—but where?

That's when Doc Broadus showed up in my life again. He had tracked me down and called my mother's home. Mom got on the telephone and shocked me with her plaintive cry to Doc. "Mr. Broadus, can you help my son? Please take him and do something—just get him out of here." I knew that my mother hated me boxing, so for her to ask Doc to do something was a major deal. Years later, Doc admitted to me, "I couldn't say no to Miss Nancy."

But if my mom's words and actions surprised me, Doc's response did almost as much. Since I didn't have the money to purchase a return plane ticket from Houston to California, Doc Broadus used his own paycheck—much to his wife's chagrin—to purchase me a one-way ticket to Oakland. By the time I got there, he already had a job lined up for me at the Job Corps in Pleasanton, where I could earn some money mopping floors and doing dishes while training in the gym during my free time.

And did we ever train! Doc worked me hard, and I was a willing student.

Eventually, I went on to the Olympic trials, where I earned the right to be the United States' heavyweight boxing representative in the 1968 Olympic Games. In Mexico City, I defeated a Russian heavyweight named Ionas Chepulis to win the Olympic gold medal. Many people still remember me as the guy who proudly strutted around the ring afterward, waving a miniature United States flag. I wanted the whole world to know that an American had won that medal.

I returned to Pleasanton as a rising star in boxing. I had all sorts of offers being thrown at me, but for a while, I remained at the Job Corps Training Center, helping to teach young men how to box. Before long, however, the center closed, and I was faced with a big decision: Should I try to make a living as a boxer, or should I do something else? I really didn't have a great desire to be a professional boxer; I just wanted to make enough money to live and to help support my mother and make a better life for my younger brothers, Roy and Kenneth. I figured that boxing would be the only way I'd ever be able to earn enough money to buy my mother a better home. About that same time, however, I met with Dick Sadler, the trainer for the former heavyweight boxing champion, Sonny Liston, who had lost his title to a loud, brash upstart named Cassius Clay, who later changed his name to Muhammad Ali. Dick and I had met the previous spring when Doc had arranged for me to be a sparring partner for Sonny as he trained for another fight.

Now, Sonny was trying to make a comeback at age thirty-seven, so I asked Dick, "Can you help me take advantage of my Olympic medal? Maybe I could do some boxing exhibitions or something?"

"Sure," Dick said. "You can travel with Sonny and fight on some of the same cards." I began training with Sonny Liston and sparring with him regularly. We became close friends—or at least as close as Sonny ever let somebody get to being his good friend. Sonny was obsessed with one thing: winning another championship. He spoke little, couldn't read, and rarely let his true thoughts and feelings be known. But I knew he trusted me, and that was all that mattered. Sonny never regained the heavyweight boxing championship belt he so passionately sought. He died at age thirty-eight.

Even after Sonny's demise, Sadler kept me on as one of his boxers. One night, almost out of the blue, Dick Sadler said, "You need to turn pro." He arranged a fight for me in Madison Square Garden, for which I received $5,000. I boxed professionally for the first time on June 23, 1969, knocking out Don Waldheim in the third round. I was on my way, knocking out one opponent after another.

With my reputation as a fierce boxer firmly established, sometimes I didn't have to work too hard for a knockout. I had to fight a young kid before I could fight Joe Frazier. The kid was a contender, but it was clear from the beginning of the fight that he was scared to death. I swung at the fellow and missed by six inches, but the fellow went reeling as though I had caught him with the full force of my fist. I swung again with all my might and missed him by two inches. Boom! The guy hit the mat and didn't get up.

"Get up!" I yelled at him.

The fellow didn't move.

The referee called a technical knockout (TKO) and declared me the winner.

I should have been happy, but I wasn't. I was mad!

Later, after the fight, I saw the boxer again.

He said, "You were really upset that I went down, weren't you?"

I said, "Yes, I was."

"You wanted me to get up, didn't you?"

"Yes!" I said emphatically.

"And you wanted to kill me."

"Yes!" I bellowed.

"That's why I didn't get up."

I worked my way up the rankings, never losing a fight. On January 22, 1973, with a record of 37 wins and no losses, I met undefeated Smokin' Joe Frazier for the heavyweight title of the world. Frazier was a formidable champion who had fought twenty-nine opponents and had knocked out twenty-five of them. He wasn't called "Smokin' Joe" for nothing. Nevertheless, the bout didn't last long. I knocked Frazier down five times before finishing him off in the second round. From my humble beginnings in Houston, I now reigned as the heavyweight champ of the world.

Along with the title and the huge championship belt came money, and lots of it. I had cars, houses, investments, you name it. The following year, I would make even more money. That's when I fought Muhammad Ali—a $5 million purse for me, which in 1974 would be something like $25 million in today's purchasing power.

MUHAMMAD ALI—STING LIKE A BEE

My much-hyped fight with Ali was to be broadcast on prime-time television via satellite. Ali's record was 44-2, with his only two losses by decision to Joe Frazier and Ken Norton, both of whom I had knocked out. My record was 40 wins, no losses, and 37 knockouts—with most of the knockouts coming in the early rounds. Although I was favored to win, two curious incidences would significantly change boxing history.

Just before the fight with Ali, my trainer handed me a glass of liquid and said, "Here's your water." That was not unusual. In fact, it was our ordinary routine for me to have a glass of water right before each bout. But this drink was not routine.

As I took a swig, I almost spit it out. "Hey, this water tastes like it has medicine in it."

"Same water as always!" he yelled defensively.

I took another drink. "Man, I *know* this water has medicine in it!"

He blurted a second time, "Same water! It's the same water as always."

I took his word for it and drank the rest. A few minutes later, I climbed into the ring with that medicinal taste still lingering in my mouth.

From the opening bell, Muhammad Ali danced around the ring, trying to elude my punches as he flicked jabs. By the end of the second round, my energy had dwindled faster than in any of my previous boxing matches. After the third round, I was as tired as if I had fought fifteen rounds. *What's going on here? Did someone slip a drug in my water?*

By the eighth round, I felt tired and weak, but I still believed I could knock out Ali if I found an opening. But Ali caught me off balance with a powerful shot to my chin, which knocked me to the canvas. Although I wasn't hurt, I waited seven seconds before I got up. When the count reached eight, I jumped to my feet. To my surprise, referee Zach Clayton quickly counted "eight-nine-ten" as one word and declared the fight over. I couldn't believe it! I had lost—my first defeat as a professional—and on a quick count.

I felt that I had been robbed of the victory, and I was furious. But I knew I could beat Ali and was determined to make a comeback to regain the title. Over the next two and a half years, I won the next five fights in a row, all by knockouts. My record now stood at 45-1, with 42 knockouts. Only one opponent stood between Muhammad Ali and me: Jimmy Young. If I could get him out of the way, I would undoubtedly get another shot at Ali.

AN UNEXPECTED CHANGE IN PLANS

My plans were rudely interrupted when the phone rang that night in December 1976. Up until then, all I thought about was my boxing career. As far as I was concerned, the entire world revolved around George Foreman. But suddenly, my world came crashing down. I loved my little nephew, George, and would do anything to see him back to normal health again.

Now I faced a foe that was too big for me to knock out, and my money couldn't buy a cure. The only hope for my nephew was a miracle, and I figured that only God—if He existed—could provide that. Common sense told me the way to contact Him was through prayer, but I had no prior experience in prayer. I didn't even know how to start. Nevertheless, I figured it was worth a shot. *Okay,* I decided. *I'm going to pray.*

Prayer, to me, was like throwing a dart up in the sky, hoping to hit something up there so I could get God's attention. After all, I was the most *unqualified* person on Earth to be praying. I was an angry, evil person. I didn't attend church, I'd never read the Bible, and I mocked and laughed at those who did. I didn't know who God was or how to talk to Him. Besides, everybody in boxing had warned me to "stay away from religion" because it would only lead to trouble. I had gladly followed their advice.

Previously, I had been curious about several religions. I knew that Muhammad Ali was a Muslim, and for a while I toyed with the idea of becoming one as well. But when he cussed me out at the boxing writers' annual banquet, where I was to receive the prestigious Fighter of the Year award and the World Boxing Association championship belt, I crossed Ali's brand of religion off my list. I thought, *If you've found religion, you've got to be at least better than me. Religion should at least make a better person out of you. I cuss a lot, but you're out-cussing me! So why would I want your religion?*

Christianity seemed boring to me—an escape for poor people and little old ladies. I wanted nothing to do with that type of religion, either.

But I didn't need religion. I needed a miracle.

I got down on my knees, feeling awkward and a little silly, but determined nonetheless.

"Okay, they say You are God . . ." I figured that was the way to start. I felt like I was just talking out loud to the air in the room. If there was no God, I was praying to nothing.

"If there is a God," I continued, "and if You really are there . . . and if You can help people . . . then please help this kid. Okay?" I got off my knees and jumped back into bed. As I lay there, for some reason, I felt that I wasn't done.

I dropped to my knees again.

"Okay, listen. This kid is having some trouble. . . ." I still wasn't sure if anyone upstairs was listening to me, but talking to God—if there was a God—was the only hope I had.

"If You really are God, and if You're up there like they say You are, if You will help this boy, I'll give up all my wealth." I paused, and then said it again for emphasis. "*All* of my wealth." I softened my tone a bit and implored, "This kid hasn't done anything with his life yet."

I figured that plea would surely catch God's ear, if He existed. I climbed back into my bed. I still couldn't sleep, so I rolled out of bed one more time and got onto my knees.

"Okay!" I roared. "Why are You messing with this kid?" I demanded, angrily challenging God. "That kid has barely started to live; he doesn't have anything; he's never gone anywhere or done anything. I've been all around the world. I've got everything. Why would You bother a poor kid like this? Take me! Take *me*! I'll give up my life instead. Just let the boy live. If You are God, *take my life!*"

I got back into bed and I fell soundly asleep, as if my prayer had finally been heard.

MIRACLES HAPPEN

The next day, the phone rang. This time I didn't care if my training got interrupted. I picked up the phone. It was my sister again, calling from the hospital.

"He woke up!" she exclaimed. "He can move his eyes, but the doctors don't think he will ever walk again."

Later that day she called again, even more excited. "He's moving his toes! But the doctors don't want us to get our hopes up. They say they still don't think he'll ever talk."

The following day she phoned with an update. "He's talking!"

Now I was getting excited. *Maybe there is a God. Maybe He has answered my prayer.*

Each day George Edward continued to improve. A week later, he was released from the hospital walking, talking, and back to normal. His doctors offered no logical explanation for his miraculous recovery. George Edward Dumas had been in critical condition, beyond human hope. But God had answered my prayer, performing a miracle of healing.

Despite such dramatic proof not only of God's existence, but of His power, it didn't take long for me to start searching for another, more plausible reason for George Edward's amazing turn-around. *There must be a natural explanation for this,* I rationalized to myself. *I know—the doctors probably made a mistake in their diagnosis. There probably wasn't anything wrong with that kid to begin with!*

"WHY ARE YOU MESSING WITH THIS KID?" I DEMANDED. "IF YOU ARE GOD, TAKE MY LIFE!"

I shucked off any thoughts about a miracle and kept living as I always had been—as "mean" George Foreman. I figured that if I could explain away the miracle, then that meant God never heard my prayer, and I was off the hook for the deal I had made with Him to take my life.

Although I didn't realize it at the time, He would hold me responsible for my part of the bargain. My days were numbered.

Round one of my life was about to end.

2
THE DAY I DIED

MARCH 1977. THREE MONTHS HAD PASSED SINCE I HAD PRAYED for my nephew's healing. Just a few days before my fight with Jimmy Young in Puerto Rico, I stood one night on the hotel balcony overlooking picturesque San Juan. As I scanned the lights of the city, I wondered about the meaning of life.

I had come a long way in my twenty-eight years, from growing up in abject poverty with never enough to eat to becoming a wealthy, well-known athlete. I had been heavyweight champion of *the world*. How many people can say that?

Yet in spite of my success, I was empty. For ten years, I had gone through the same routine in preparing for a fight—running, sparring, and getting in shape. But in the end, after all that effort, the most I could get for it was another win on my boxing record. That was my goal in life—getting another "W." I thought, *Is that all there is to life?*

Money didn't fill the void. I had more cash in my accounts than most people could ever dream of. My assets included three homes, a dozen cars, and a ranch—yet even with all that stuff, I was still unfulfilled. Would another car make me happy? One more house? Some mysterious piece of the puzzle was missing, but I didn't know what it was or where to find it.

More than once I toyed with the idea of driving my car over a cliff. I desperately needed help, but I wasn't about to set up an appointment with a psychiatrist. Only crazy people went to shrinks, and, of course, I didn't want anyone to think I was nuts!

IN SPITE OF MY SUCCESS, I WAS EMPTY.

Even though I wanted nothing to do with religion, I still believed that a God existed. Although I wasn't sure if He could hear me, I again called out to Him like I had done in Marshall, Texas, for my nephew.

"God, if You're real, maybe You can use me as something more than a boxer."

There, I said it. The offer was on the table—and if He really existed, He could take it or leave it.

My prayer would soon be answered in a way that I never could have imagined.

THE FIGHT OF MY LIFE

The day arrived for my twelve-round bout with Jimmy Young. Excitement filled the air as I glanced around at the sold-out stadium. Just before the fight was to begin, promoter Don King came over to my corner. Known for his wild hairstyle and even wilder personality, Don was also a shrewd businessman. "George, the crowd's a sellout and the ratings are going to be great," Don told me, shaking my hand as he looked up into my eyes. "Just don't knock him out too early."

I knew what he meant. Everyone would make more money if the fight lasted longer. If I knocked him out in the early rounds, as I had done to most of my opponents, the television networks couldn't sell their ads. Don wanted me to extend the fight to allow the networks time to run as many commercials as possible. I figured that I would eventually knock out Jimmy Young just as I had so many other opponents, so I could easily delay the inevitable for a few rounds. Not a problem.

I played around with Jimmy for the first two rounds, then delivered a punch that stunned him in round three. One of my trainers, Charley Shipes, yelled, "Now, George! Do it now!" Even though I knew I could put him away, I remembered Don King's advice to prolong the fight. I let Jimmy off the hook, thinking I could end the fight after a few more rounds.

My mercy backfired, as Young gained a shot of confidence by surviving the round. He managed to avoid my punches for several more rounds while delivering a few good ones of his own.

By the seventh round, I figured it was time to get this fight over. I hit him with a shot that buckled his knees. Again, I thought about the television networks and wondered if I had waited long enough. And again I backed off. Young was able to escape my attacks and survived another round. Later, in an interview with *Sports Illustrated*, Young admitted the fight could have ended right then. "All he had to do to win was push me with his little finger."

By now, the crowd was solidly behind Jimmy. Muhammad Ali's fans during his fights would repeatedly yell, "A-lee, A-lee, A-lee!" After Young endured my attacks, the spectators started chanting choruses of "Jim-mee, Jim-mee . . ."

In the twelfth and final round, I believed I was ahead on points, but a knockout would guarantee me the victory. As I began chasing him around the ring, I threw a wild punch off balance. He caught me at just the right time and knocked me down. Immediately I jumped back up, letting the judges know that I wasn't hurt. But Jimmy was already ahead on two of the judges' scorecards, and that knockdown sealed the outcome.

When the final bell rang, I was still confident I had won. I could hardly believe it when the announcer raised Young's hand and declared him the winner. By being merciful to my opponent, I had inadvertently handed the win over to him.

What happened next took me by even greater surprise.

NOT READY TO DIE

Upon hearing the judges' decision, I hastily returned to my hot, stuffy dressing room—the place where I was supposed to "cool down." Joining me in the room were my trainers, Gil Clancy and Charley Shipes, physician Dr. Keith West, equipment manager John Fowlkes, masseur Perry Fuller, bodyguard Lamar, and my brothers Roy and Sonny.

The building's air-conditioning had gone out that night, and the intense heat was smothering me. I've never been so hot in all my life! Large drops of perspiration streamed down my face and chest. But I was also energized, still running on adrenalin. I paced back and forth in the room, like a racehorse trying to cool down.

Wiping the sweat off my face, I hollered, "Man, it's hot in here! Somebody open a window!" But the room had no windows except for a small vent over the door that somebody cracked open. It didn't help the air flow one bit.

As I kept pacing back and forth, I reflected on the fight and my future. *I lost the fight. That's no big thing. I'm George Foreman. I can do television and movies. I've got money to travel. I've got everything I want. I could go home right now to my nice ranch and retire.*

And die.

And die? Where did that come from? The statement seemed to come out of nowhere, like a bomb dropped on an unsuspecting victim. Dying was the last thing on my mind.

I've got everything to live for, I convinced myself. *I've got my expensive cars and houses. I have money in the bank, money in a safety-deposit box, and I've got a big ranch. Who needs boxing? I can retire right now.*

And die.

And die? WHY DO I KEEP THINKING ABOUT DYING?

I looked around the room, wondering where that voice was coming from. I figured the walls must be speaking to me! I tried again to shake off the negative image in my mind.

I've got too much to live for. I don't want to die. I don't care about this stupid boxing match. I could walk away from this right now. I've got a contract with a television network to make movies, and I could retire right now.

The ominous words came again: *And die.*

Die! This was the third time that word intruded on my mind, but it was not coming from me.

I had heard about boxers dying after big fights. Was I next? *That's not going to happen to me!* I assured myself. *I'm not depressed. I'm okay.*

Just then, a voice interrupted my thoughts.

You believe in God. Why are you afraid to die?

Where did that voice come from? Was that God talking to me? Yeah, I believed in God. I just didn't believe in religion. I knew that somebody made the sun, moon, and stars, but I hated going to church, hearing all those pitiful old songs people sang, and using words like "thee" and "thou." I didn't believe in all *that*. I thought religion was just for poor people. It wasn't for me, because I was rich.

The voice spoke again: *If you believe in God, why are you afraid to die?*

Now I *was* scared. In fact, I had never been so afraid in all my life! A few months before, I had prayed in my bedroom for God to take my life if He would heal my nephew. I never dreamed He would actually take me up on it.

I continued to pace back and forth even faster. I was fighting to keep myself alive because I knew death was staring me in the face. I reminisced about some favorite things that had happened during my life, recalling them like a video tape running fast-forward, as though I knew somehow that it was about to end.

By now I was crying. I decided I wanted to make a deal with God. My mind was racing, hurriedly trying to figure out what I could do on my part. *What does a mere human being own that he can use to barter with God? I'm still George Foreman*, I thought. *I can still box. I can give money to charities. I can give to cancer charities....*

The voice thundered, *I don't want your money. I want YOU!*

I knew that couldn't be a human voice, because every human I knew wanted money. This voice turned down my money! I believed in God, but I didn't want to die. My body was toned perfectly, and I had everything in life the way I wanted it. I wasn't ready to die at such a young age.

Finally, I said, "God, I believe in You—but not enough to die."

I felt sure that my life was about to end, and amazingly one thing troubled me more deeply than anything else. It wasn't fear of hell or disappointment at missing heaven. It bothered me that I didn't have a chance to say good-bye to my mother. My mother had been so good to me; she had believed in me even when there was nothing to believe in. But that's what mothers do. They believe despite the odds. Now I knew that I was about to leave this world, and I felt sad that I didn't at least have an opportunity to express my thanks to her for all she had sacrificed for me. *I wish I'd have had a chance to say good-bye*, I thought.

At that moment, I felt my legs buckle and I collapsed, pitching forward toward the floor. I could feel myself falling and I yelled to the others in the room, "Hey, I'm fixing to—" Before I could finish my sentence, I was gone.

TRANSPORTED INTO DARKNESS

Instantly I was transported into a deep, dark void, like a bottomless pit. If there's a place called "nowhere," this was it. I was suspended in emptiness, with nothing over my head or under my feet. I lost my perception of direction, and didn't know which way was up and which way was down. This was a place of total isolation, cut off from everything and everyone. It can only be described as a vacant space of extreme hopelessness, like being dropped in the Atlantic Ocean with nothing to grab on to, a thousand miles from the shore.

I knew I was dead, and this wasn't heaven. I was terrified, knowing I had no way out. Sorrow beyond description engulfed my soul, more than anyone could ever imagine. If you multiplied every disturbing and frightening thought that you've ever had during your entire life, that wouldn't come close to the panic I felt.

Total darkness surrounded me. I was drifting like an astronaut cut off from his spacecraft, all alone in the complete darkness of outer space—but with no planets, moons, or stars as light or reference points. Even that would be better than where I was. Although I couldn't see anyone, I was aware of other people in this terrible place. I was unable to contact them, because in this void where there was no light, I sensed that relationships didn't exist.

The place reeked with the putrid smell of death. It's difficult to describe the awful, foul stench. If you've ever been to a dump yard and smelled the decaying odors, just multiply that stomach-wrenching smell a thousand times. You can't forget it. The offensive odor was so revolting that I still vividly remember it to this day.

Everything that I ever worked for—my money, cars, and houses— meant nothing to me anymore. What good were they to me here? No earthly fortune can satisfy someone who is trapped in solitary confinement and can't see anything. It was utter darkness. This place was a vacuum without light, love, or happiness. I was so frightened that I didn't want even my worst enemies to experience it. No one ever could have done anything to me that was so bad that I wished them to come here.

I couldn't compare my feelings of hopelessness to any earthly experience. It wasn't like a temporary jail sentence, where one day I'd be let out. I couldn't say, "This is the worst place imaginable, but I can get out of here tomorrow, or next week, or next month." In that place, I had no hope for tomorrow—or of ever getting out.

I truly thought that this was the end of my life, and I saw—too late—that I had missed what life was meant to be about. As that realization dawned on me, I got mad; I mean, I was furious that I had fallen for the devil's lies and deceptions. I screamed with every ounce of strength in me, "I don't care if this *is* death. I still believe there's a God!"

> **I KNEW I WAS DEAD, AND THIS WASN'T HEAVEN.**

Instantly, what seemed to be like a gigantic hand reached down and snatched me out of the terrifying place. Immediately I was back inside my body in the dressing room. I couldn't believe it; I wasn't in darkness anymore! Even though I had lost all hope of escaping, God had mercifully let me out!

BACK IN MY BODY

When my legs buckled beneath me, I had collapsed on the floor. Apparently, my brothers and trainer had picked me up and laid my body on the training table. Now I was alive again. I could *feel* the blood running through my veins. All fear of dying had disappeared. The worst thing that could have happened to me *had* happened to me. Yet for some reason, I was alive!

The men in the dressing room gathered around the table—my brothers Sonny and Roy, Charley Shipes, Gil Clancy, Lamar, and Perry Fuller—all of them staring at me, their mouths wide open in astonishment. All except Perry, who was sobbing, the tears streaming down his face. I still thought I was dying, but since the fear of death was gone, I was almost cheerful. "Hey,

I'm dying," I said, "but tell everybody that I'm dying for God!" I knew it had been God's hand that rescued me out of that dark place. I lay back on the table, expecting to die at any moment, but this time, I wasn't afraid. I wasn't tormented by the fear of death anymore. I was at peace with God and at peace with myself.

All my life, in spite of my money and accomplishments, I had never felt fulfilled or truly happy. I continually wanted to go to new places; I always wanted to be somewhere else. I envied those who seemed to be more successful, wishing I could be in their shoes. But what occurred next totally flushed that discontentment out of me.

As I lay on the table, my spirit inside me was suddenly yanked from one place to another, like I was riding on a roller coaster. My stomach floated, like when a coaster goes up over a hump and then lurches downward. Instantly in my mind, I was shown all the places I had dreamed of going. I felt what it was like to be in the shoes of the people I had admired so immensely—Sammy Davis Jr., and other celebrities. But just when I settled at being in each place and living that person's life, I was immediately yanked up and taken to another place to be a different person.

Not only did I sense the success and failure of my heroes; I also experienced the practice of every religion of these people. Nothing satisfied. This weird "virtual-reality tour" seemed to last for hours, but it couldn't have been but for a few moments in real time.

Finally, in frustration I cried out, "I'm George Foreman! I just lost that boxing match. I don't care where You're taking me—I lost the fight, and I'm who I want to be. I don't want to be anyone else!"

The moment those words left my lips, the journey stopped, and I opened my eyes.

JESUS CHRIST IS REVEALED TO ME

Dr. Keith West was standing behind me and instinctively grabbed my head to support it. I felt his strong fingertips, but I sensed something far beyond his grip, and I saw something that nearly caused my heart to stop, not in fear, but in amazement. I said, "Dr. West, please move your hands, because the thorns on His head are making Him bleed." I reached up and touched my forehead. When I did, I saw blood pouring down my forehead, yet I didn't have a cut there from the boxing match.

Prior to this incident, I had thought the crucifixion of Christ was a fictional television story people watched at Easter time. I hadn't gone to church enough to know much about it. I joked about people who believed in such nonsense. In fact, I always believed that Joe Frazier was tough, until I saw him holding a Bible one day before a fight. I was disgusted at the sight. *That is a weakness,* I thought.

On the other hand, my masseur, Perry Fuller, often shared Scriptures with me when we were alone or when nobody else was paying attention to us. Most members of my team avoided conversations with Perry because he was always talking about "religion." Months before, while he was working on me one day, Perry spoke in his deep, raspy, gravel-toned voice, "Mr. Foreman, I want to read to you a passage from the Bible. It's from the forty-ninth Psalm." Perry didn't wait for my permission; he simply started reading: "'They that trust in their wealth . . . they call their lands after their own names . . . they shall be *consumed in the grave.*" Perry paused long enough to move around to the front of the training table where he looked me right in the eyes. "You see, Mr. Foreman, you can't trust in your wealth." Perry was letting me know in his own words that my money would be no good after I died and that I needed to put my trust in God.

Now, in that hot dressing room in Puerto Rico, this man, who had told me about the Lord, was an eyewitness to my transformation. Perry was crying as he held down my hands. No doubt, he had never seen anything like this. I said, "Mr. Fuller, move your hands. He's bleeding where they crucified Him." I looked at both of my hands and saw them bleeding, but no one else in the room could see it. Instead, they all looked at me as if I'd lost my mind—everyone, even Perry. Although he may have understood more than any of us what was going on.

To this day, I can't figure out why I said "He" when this experience was happening to *me.* I have no idea why I could see the blood but the others in the room could not. I believed in God, but I didn't believe in religion. Now God was revealing Himself to me in a way I would never forget. He wasn't simply one of many gods. God was showing me that Jesus truly did bleed while wearing that crown of thorns and when they pounded those nails into His hands—and although I didn't completely understand it, and certainly didn't deserve such a sacrifice, I was beginning to realize that He did it for me.

I later found out about a man in the Bible named Saul, who was as hard-headed as I was. He didn't believe in Jesus either. One day, Saul was traveling on a road to Damascus when the Lord struck him down with a blinding light, and a voice from heaven spoke to him. Saul became a completely different man after that experience, and his name was changed to Paul. The people traveling with him didn't understand what was happening to him any more than the guys in my dressing room could comprehend what I was experiencing.[1]

Still lying prone on the training table, I suddenly sat straight up and yelled at the top of my voice, "JESUS CHRIST IS COMING ALIVE IN ME!"

That's when all the faces in the room turned ashen, as if they had seen a ghost. Prior to this experience, I had never talked about religion. I was your typical tough guy—and in my world, tough guys didn't talk about Jesus. But something stirred inside me, in the lower part of my stomach, and I could no longer control what I was saying.

I started reciting Scriptures from the Bible—even though I had never learned them. For most of my life, I had been ruled by anger and hatred. Now, every hostile emotion had been drained out of me, and a spigot of God's love had been turned on inside me, filling me up, and overflowing out of me.

I jumped up off the table and hugged everyone in the room, telling them that I loved them. I grabbed Gil Clancy, who always talked about his Irish heritage. I kissed him and said, "Gil, I love you! You're my brother!" (I *never* would have done that before as the old George, but a supernatural force had taken hold of me.) In all those years together, I had never told any of my closest associates that I loved them. Now, I couldn't stop expressing how much I loved them.

Half joking, my brother, Roy, suggested that I needed to clean up. I couldn't have agreed with him more. I already felt spiritually clean on the inside, but I wanted my physical body to be cleansed, too. But because the showers didn't have any warm water, my trainer worried that the cold water might send me into shock. "Don't let him shower yet! Don't let him go in there!" He called out to the others to stop me. All eight men tried to hold me back, but I pushed through them, stepped into the small shower stall, and turned on the water.

And then I heard myself speaking words that I had never before used. Standing in the shower I shouted, "Hallelujah, I'm clean! HALLELUJAH, I'VE BEEN BORN AGAIN!" I yelled like a kid who had just hit a home run and won the big game. "I've got to go tell the whole world about this!"

I stepped out of the shower and, still naked, headed toward the front door. The men in the room wrestled me down; they had to sit on me to keep me from going outside. "George! Take it easy," I heard one of them say. "Calm down, man," somebody else added. "There are hundreds of people right outside that door. You can't go out there, George."

> **I YELLED AT THE TOP OF MY VOICE, "JESUS CHRIST IS COMING ALIVE IN ME!"**

"Jesus Christ is coming alive in me!" I responded. "I love you! God loves you!" The guys in the room—most of whom had known me for years—didn't know what to think. Dr. West actually had tears in his eyes, not tears of joy, but tears of pity. This was so out of character for me. I wouldn't stop talking about Jesus, and no one could shut me up. Now I was praising the name of Jesus, the name my acquaintances had only heard me use in profanity.

As for me, I had never felt that wonderful in all my life! This born-again experience was everything I ever wanted. I didn't know such feelings of joy and euphoria were possible this side of heaven, and I didn't know that heaven even existed. The thrill of being introduced as the heavyweight champion of the world didn't even come close to this.

As the men held me down, I heard the voice bid me farewell.

I come to My brothers and they don't believe Me. I come to My friends and they don't understand Me.

"Wait!" I yelled. "Don't let Jesus go! Don't let Jesus go!" (as if the men in the room could actually do anything to prevent His departure).

I didn't want Him to leave. Again I pleaded, "Don't let Jesus go!"

Now I go to My Father in heaven.

And with those words, my experience ended.

FINALLY FINDING PEACE

But the peace remained. For the first time in my life, I could honestly say I was at peace. At that moment, I felt like a giant on top of the world. I finally had it all—happiness, significance, contentment. Just minutes before, I had been more terrified than at any other time in my life. God had allowed me to experience the absolute worst feeling—and the absolute best—all within a matter of minutes.

Years before, a friend told me, "George, one day you're going to have it all. You'll have money, fleets of cars. . . ." I envisioned everything he was describing. "Wow," I replied, "I'm going to feel good when that happens."

My childhood hero, football sensation Jim Brown, once came to my ranch to do a television interview with me. I always wanted to be just like Jim. By now, I was a successful world champion boxer and my idol actually came to my house. After gawking at my manicured lawn, beautiful home, and exquisite furniture, Jim Brown said, "George, you've got it made. I just hope one day I can get it together like you."

Get it together like me? I was trying to get it together like him!

But after I acquired all the money, cars, and other playthings that often accompany great accomplishments, the good feeling I was waiting for never came. I was still empty. I kept looking for whatever it was that would fulfill me. The title heavyweight champion of the world didn't do it. Fame didn't satisfy. Fancy cars and houses didn't do it for me. A million dollars didn't do it. But when I had my encounter with God in San Juan, I found what I had been looking for all my life. I finally had it made!

I told my team that day, "Y'all have just witnessed a miracle, and you're not going to believe it."

Dr. West immediately tried to explain away what he had seen and heard with his own eyes and ears. "George, you just got your bell rung," he said. The implication was obvious—"You'll get over this religious stuff in a short while, George, after you come to your senses."

I laugh now when I think about that. I guess Dr. West had forgotten that I didn't get knocked out. I hadn't gotten my "bell rung." I had gone the full twelve rounds, and Jimmy Young won on the judges' scorecards. What had happened to me didn't have a natural explanation, so a shot to the head was the best answer the good doctor could come up with.

Just moments before in that Puerto Rican dressing room, I was a man who didn't believe in the Bible. I had rejected all religion. Jesus was merely a cussword to me. I didn't love anybody but myself. After my divine encounter, however, I knew that I was a completely different man.

I didn't "imagine" going to that frightening, dark place. I *went* there. It was *real*. I *saw* the blood on my hands. I *heard* the voice speaking to me. I quoted Scriptures I didn't even know. And amazingly, I was now praising Jesus instead of using His name in profanity.

All of my hate—and I had hated a lot of people—was gone. God's love flowed through me to others in a way that, frankly, I can't adequately understand or express. Every attitude and emotion in me had flip-flopped. How could anyone explain the switch from night to day that had taken place in me? It was nothing short of a miracle.

I now felt like I was *someone*—a person who really mattered. Ironically, I had never really felt significant before. Even when I was the heavyweight champion of the world, I was just faking it—putting on an act as though I felt good about myself. But in that dressing room, God opened my spiritually blind eyes and introduced Himself to me. Think about that: He came looking for *me*; the Almighty condescended to encounter me! No experience on Earth could make me feel more important than that.

A MEDIA FRENZY

Dr. West suggested that I should be taken from my dressing room to the hospital for observation. The men in the training room strapped me down on a stretcher. I knew that I was okay—better, in fact, than I'd ever been. At the hospital, the doctors checked me over but couldn't find anything wrong. Nevertheless, they encouraged me to stay overnight as a precautionary measure.

The next day, the media was scrambling to find out what had happened in that dressing room, which seemed to be bigger news than the fight itself. Word had leaked out and every reporter wanted to get the scoop.

Gil Clancy, my publicity-savvy trainer, said to me, "George, everybody's going to be asking you what happened. Tell them that you had heat prostration."

"Heat what?" I had never heard of the word before.

"Prostration," he said. "Now learn to say it."

I rehearsed the word. "Pros-tra-shun."

"Good, now try it again."

"Heat prostration. Heat prostration. Heat prostration!"

Gil said, "Okay. We'll let the reporters in your room now."

When the reporters walked in the room, I wanted to get the word out of the way, so I yelled, "Heat prostration!"

"What's that?" one reporter asked.

Before I had a chance to say anything, Gil interrupted and gave his explanation of what he thought had happened to me.

PERMANENT CHANGE

It's been three decades since my experience in that Puerto Rican dressing room, but it's just as real to me today as the day it happened. I don't remember many of the details about my fight in Zaire with Ali. It's pretty much out of my mind. Even though I regained the heavyweight boxing title in 1994, I can't remember much about it. But I'll never forget what happened in that dressing room in 1977. Every detail remains vivid to me.

I've been trying to live in that moment for the last thirty years. I'll never forget it. But those men in the dressing room who witnessed my conversion—it's the oddest thing—they never talk about it. Over the years, whenever I've tried discussing it with them, they quickly change the subject. To me, it's strange that they aren't curious about it and don't want to know more. One thing they can't deny is that I've been a different man ever since that day.

Round one, the first twenty-eight years of my life, was a charade. That was behind me. Now, I was ready to begin round two—my second chance at life.

3
GET ME A HIT MAN

ON MY FLIGHT BACK FROM PUERTO RICO, I COULDN'T HELP BUT wonder what the future held for me. I was still trying to sort out what it all meant. What did God want with my life, and what was I supposed to do next? My experience in San Juan had opened my eyes to another world, beyond the grave. I had tasted death and visited the dark realm on the other side.

What exactly was that place that I went to? I don't know for sure; I wish I could tell you. I know it wasn't hell, but perhaps it was a glimpse of what eternity without God must be like. I still shudder every time I think of it. I was never afraid to climb into the boxing ring to fight, but I was terrified every moment I spent in that other world. The foul, rotten odor was worse than any stench on Earth, like inhaling death and not being able to exhale. I didn't want *anyone* to go to there, not even my worst enemy.

Before my death experience, I had a lot of enemies. I *hated* Muhammad Ali. I had never despised anyone more than that man. After I lost my heavyweight title to him, I would have loved nothing more than to kill him in the boxing ring. That would have given me revenge on Ali and respect in the boxing world. It may seem unreasonable or maybe even ridiculous to someone who comes from a background different from mine, or to someone who has never been immersed in a sport or obsessed with an activity, but malicious, destructive thoughts such as those filled my mind and, in a strange, indirect way, motivated me.

I'm going to kill that Muhammad Ali with my fists. He took my heavyweight title. I'm going to kill this guy. I'm going to show that promoter, and the people in Africa, and the people in New York . . .

Hate flowed through me like adrenaline. At times, I actually considered hiring a hit man to take out a few people. They had done some things to me that I thought were unforgivable, so I believed I could justify my reasons for getting even.

After one person stole some money from me, I thought, *I think I'm going to get me a hit man.* When a couple of guys double-crossed me, hiring a hit man entered my mind again. Of course, I never did, but the thought was there often. A few other people did some bad things to me, and the idea came pounding back. *I want to kill these people. I need to get me a hit man.*

I had the money to make it happen. My only problem would be pulling it off. It was no secret that I hated those guys, so I would immediately become a suspect if they mysteriously died. Day and night, I considered every scheme imaginable to get them bumped off without arousing suspicion. *How could I have them killed and not have anyone think that I did it?*

Sadly, an assassin can be found all too easily, if you hint around to enough people. But covering your tracks is another story. I backed away from hiring a hit man, not because I had any moral qualms about killing at that time, but simply because I couldn't figure out how to get away with it. Whenever I watched a television show where someone hired a hit man, the cops always caught the bad guy! The threat of going to prison was enough to keep me from doing it, and I thank God that I never followed through with my plans. Nevertheless, I admit the feelings were there.

Maybe you've had similar thoughts about someone who has hurt you. You might not have actually considered hiring a hit man, but perhaps you have harbored evil thoughts and intentions, hoping your enemy would die. Maybe you secretly wished he or she would meet with an unfortunate accident. It's the same attitude as wanting to hire an assassin. It's the spirit of revenge; you want the other person to pay dearly for what he or she did to you.

But do you really think that getting revenge will fix your problems? It didn't for me. I discovered that God has a better plan. It's called forgiveness, and I strongly recommend it to you. Forgiving others is the only way you'll ever find peace of mind.

MY MOST URGENT ASSIGNMENT

You'd think that telling the world about my death experience might be the first thing God would want me to do. It wasn't. When I "died," I regretted that I hadn't said good-bye to my mother or to anyone in my family. Now that I was back among the living, I felt that I was getting another chance to do that. Upon my arrival back home, the first thing I did was to go to my mother's house to tell her that I loved her. I felt compelled to tell my family, friends, and even my enemies how much I loved them.

Besides expressing love, expressing forgiveness became a priority to me. After God snatched me out of that dark place, I completely forgave everyone I had ever hated. It was my wake-up call. I'm not exaggerating when I tell you that you don't want even your worst enemy to go there. I've been there! The enemy I needed to forgive the most was a friend who had betrayed me.

I met Leroy Jackson during my days in the Job Corps, before I started boxing. We were both poor at that time and both trying to figure out what we were going to do with

I ACTUALLY CONSIDERED HIRING A HIT MAN TO TAKE OUT A FEW PEOPLE.

our lives. After I started boxing professionally, I gave him the best opportunity he had ever had in his life: I asked him to come work for me as one of my managers. He was my manager for the Joe Frazier fight when I won the heavyweight title, and Leroy worked for me through the Ali fight. I assumed he appreciated all I had done for him, and so I trusted him.

One day I got word from my accountants that some items were missing out of my financial portfolio. I was shocked to find out that Leroy Jackson had sold my home in California without my knowledge. But it wasn't just my house that he had put up for sale. He also sold all of its contents at an auction and kept the money for himself!

Every piece of beautiful handmade furniture was gone. All of my collectibles and souvenirs that I had brought back from Japan, Africa, and other countries, which were worth many thousands of dollars, had been sold. And to top it off, he got rid of my personal memorabilia that I couldn't put a price tag on—family items, pictures, and trophies.

But my most prized possession, the one that meant the most to me, was the pair of boxing gloves that I had used to win the heavyweight championship. It was my proof that I had won the title. Leroy sold those priceless boxing gloves as well.

Losing those gloves hurt me the most. I had envisioned showing them to my children and grandchildren when I got older, telling the story about those gloves. Now they were nowhere to be found. (Later, when I won the title the second time, God restored to me a new pair of championship gloves.)

My brother went to the house to investigate and called me with more bad news. "George, I hate to tell you this, but they've stripped the house of everything and have even ripped out the wallpaper!"

Leroy had stolen my money, my material possessions, and personal items that I had hoped to pass down to my posterity, and he thought he could get away with it. I just couldn't understand it. How could he steal those things from me? I was one of the few friends he had in the whole world. I had given him a big break in life; in return, he stabbed me in the back.

I was so angry at Leroy, I would have done almost anything to have gotten even—and I seriously considered hiring a hit man. Just before I went to Puerto Rico to fight Jimmy Young, I tried to track down Leroy, but I couldn't find him. The authorities eventually caught Leroy, and a court date was set for after my return to the United States. Then it would be my turn to get even.

What I wasn't counting on was my conversion experience in Puerto Rico, which would change my heart forever—including how I would deal with my enemies. After my encounter with God in that dressing room in March 1977, my whole life turned upside down. God flushed all aggression and hatred out of my heart, like rinsing the filth out of a septic tank.

Because I no longer had hate boiling within me, I couldn't imagine boxing again. I couldn't even make a fist to hit a punching bag. I could no longer view my opponents as animals to be hunted, but as human beings—the most valuable of God's creation. Having a new compassion for my enemies kindled an obsession within me to mend my damaged relationships.

Later in 1977, I was staying in a hotel in San Francisco. Leroy was going to trial and was there at the same hotel to meet with my attorneys. As soon as I walked into the hotel lobby, I spotted Leroy walking my way. When he saw me, he gasped in sheer terror, as if he'd seen somebody who was supposed to be dead—and in a way, he had. He knew the old George Foreman always sought revenge, and he probably assumed that I would kill him right there in the lobby.

I quickly closed the distance between us, making sure he couldn't get away. I walked over to him, flashed a broad smile, and to his surprise, gave him a big bear hug. "I want you to know that I love you, Leroy," I said, like a father talking to a son. "Everything's okay. We all make mistakes. That was then, but this is now. I forgive you for everything you did to me."

Leroy was so stunned, he could barely speak. He mumbled a bunch of words that didn't connect into a sentence. He just couldn't understand my attitude. He had only known me as someone filled with rage, but now he had met the new George. I wasn't the same person he had known before. Even though he still had to go to court the next day and stand

> **I WAS ONE OF THE FEW FRIENDS HE HAD IN THE WHOLE WORLD. I HAD GIVEN HIM A BIG BREAK IN LIFE; IN RETURN, HE STABBED ME IN THE BACK.**

trial on some serious charges, I wanted him to know that I didn't hate him anymore for what he had done. When I embraced him, I got more relief out of it than he did. I felt sorry for him, and in a sense, I was partially responsible for his downfall. Maybe I put him in a position he wasn't capable of handling; perhaps I should have built in some better systems of accountability in our management team. Maybe if I had kept closer tabs on him, he wouldn't have stolen from me. I know every person has to take responsibility for his or her own actions, so while Leroy faced up to his, I wanted to be sure I faced my part too.

CONTACTING MY ENEMIES

Leroy wasn't the only one I needed to forgive. I had dozens of broken relationships that needed rebuilding. I felt compelled to call every one of my enemies to ask for their forgiveness and for a chance to start over. Even if they wanted nothing to do with me, I was determined to do everything possible to make things right.

For the next two months, calling those people became my highest priority. I tried to phone every person I had hurt to explain what had happened to me. God had given me a second chance at life, and this was my opportunity to do it right this time.

HE WAS STUNNED. I WASN'T THE SAME PERSON THAT HE HAD KNOWN BEFORE.

Some of the people I had offended had moved and were hard to find. In those days, we didn't have the Internet, where I could just get online and look up an address and phone number. I had to flip through pages in phone books and make numerous calls to the information operator. Sometimes I would call the wrong number, which was the same name as the individual I was hunting down, but it wouldn't be the right person.

When I finally made a connection, the conversation was understandably awkward at times. I usually started the conversation lightheartedly before relating the account of what happened to me in the dressing room in Puerto Rico and how God had changed my life. Then I'd say, "I want to ask your forgiveness for hurting you. You didn't do anything to me. The past is gone, so let's move on. I don't hate you anymore. I love you."

Most of them were suspicious, thinking I had ulterior motives. Some would defensively ask, "Why are you calling me? Why are you telling me this?"

I heard a lot of that. They thought I was trying to trick them because my suggestion to forgive and forget made no sense to them. Maybe they'd never heard anyone truly ask forgiveness before, so they didn't know how to respond.

Some people didn't want to deal with the issues, and I could instantly feel it from them. They'd say, "Why do you want to bother me again? Just leave me alone!"

When someone refused to talk with me, I told myself, *Maybe he's not ready to talk right now. I'll try him again later.* This was *my* chance to get things straight. Those people didn't owe me anything. I was indebted to them and wasn't expecting anything in return.

I believed that God had given me a temporary reprieve, that He was granting me an extension on life so I could get right with everyone before I died again. I assumed that I wasn't going to live much longer. When you have what they call a "near-death experience" like I did, you don't have a real firm grasp on life anymore. I still view life as extremely fragile. It's like a feather floating around. I could die at any moment. In case I passed away, I wanted each of my enemies to know that I sincerely cared about them. I didn't want anything bad to happen to them. And whatever we did to each other in the past—it was now over, as far as I was concerned.

It took me more than two years to locate all of the people I had hurt, and I may have missed a few. For me, getting right with people I hurt or offended goes on to this day. Every now and then I'll think of someone else or run into a person I had forgotten about. When I encounter someone like that, I do my best to apologize and make things right. It's not always possible, but I'm committed to trying to restore broken relationships.

I needed to make amends with a former girlfriend who loved me dearly and thought we would get married. She was a wonderful girl and came from a good family, but I wasn't interested in or ready for marriage at the time. After we broke up, she told my mother, "Tell George not to throw away what we had."

But I did.

Following my conversion, I asked her forgiveness for the way I had treated her.

"There was nothing wrong with you," I said. "I had big problems back then. You were okay. It was *me* that was messed up. Please forgive me for hurting you." I wanted to make sure she knew that I was telling the truth so we could both move on with our lives.

I phoned many people who had worked for me. I hated my former manager, Dick Sadler, so I called him to patch things up. I talked with at least ten people with whom I had serious issues. I even went back to my old neighborhood where I grew up. I sat on the porch with some of my old friends and apologized for ignoring them after I became famous.

"I'm sorry I didn't remember you after all you did to help me get ahead," I'd say. "Thank you for being in my life when I needed you." I helped some of them financially to show my appreciation. Sometimes I just sat and listened to them. I wanted everyone to know that I really appreciated their being in my life. I had never before expressed that to them.

Not everyone wanted to get right with me. Some of my enemies never wanted to see my face again. But that's okay. I couldn't force them to do anything, and whether they ever decide to forgive me is between them and God. I did my part in trying to repair the relationship, which made me a free man. God had shown me mercy, and I shared that same mercy with others.

YOUR OPPORTUNITY

Perhaps you're wondering why we need to forgive. You're saying, "George, you just don't understand what this person did to me. I can't forgive because I'm still hurting too much."

What that person did to you may have been wrong, and your hurting is real as a result. But that's exactly why you must forgive. If no one did anything wrong, you wouldn't need to forgive. If you weren't wounded, you wouldn't need to be healed. But the pain won't go away until you pardon the person and let go of the hurt.

> WHENEVER YOU GO TO BED, THE INVISIBLE PERSON GETS IN BED WITH YOU, KEEPING YOU AWAKE ALL NIGHT.

Unforgiveness will eat you up inside and drain your life of all happiness. Whenever you sit down to eat a nice breakfast, the person you hate pops into your mind. You can't enjoy your meal because you're thinking about what he did to you. The rest of your day is ruined because your enemy is living inside your mind.

If you go on a paddleboat ride to relax, you can't row two strokes without thinking, *I can't believe she betrayed me like that. I'll never forgive her!* Meanwhile, the woman you hate is oblivious to the fact. The only one who's suffering is you.

When you go on vacation, you don't leave the unforgiven person behind. You take him along, and he sits next to you during the entire trip. Whenever you go to bed, the invisible person gets in bed with you, keeping you awake all night. You toss and turn because you can't get your enemy out of your mind. You can't rest. You can't enjoy your meals. You can't take pleasure in anything. All because you won't forgive.

THE PAIN WON'T GO AWAY UNTIL YOU PARDON THE PERSON AND LET GO OF THE HURT.

It's a miserable way to live, isn't it? Nevertheless, millions of people have never figured it out. They've locked up people in the jailhouse of their mind and won't let them out. And the prisoners are rioting inside! That's why some people have no peace of mind. They prefer to live in constant torment, rather than set their prisoners free. That's the way I used to be until I forgave all the people who offended me.

THE SECRET TO FORGIVING OTHERS

The truth is, I couldn't forgive my enemies before I met God. I didn't have the willpower within me to do it. It just wasn't natural, or logical, to let those who wronged me off the hook. Unless He did it through me, it wasn't going to happen. The good Lord had to put His supernatural love inside my heart before I could express it through forgiveness.

When God saved me in Puerto Rico, He removed all hatred from my heart. I no longer felt the need to hire a hit man because I didn't hate anymore. God's forgiveness removed my rage, and I know it can remove your hate, too. Forgiveness will heal your hurt and your heart. When you forgive, you'll release the prisoners from your self-made jailhouse.

Forgiveness proceeds out of compassion, not anger. To forgive someone, you must view your enemy with compassion. You have to see them through the eyes of pity. Jesus told a story about a slave who owed a king millions of dollars in today's currency. The king forgave him of that debt, but only after he *felt compassion* for him.[1]

Understand, there's a bigger issue than the one you're upset about. Perhaps your enemy doesn't know God. That's a bigger issue. When I died and went to that horrible dark place, compassion became a bigger issue for me than all of the hurt that I had experienced at the hands of other people. I didn't want my enemies to go there, so my compassion outweighed everything they had done to me. It moved me to have pity on them and overshadowed every hurt that I had ever suffered. What they had done to me was so trivial in comparison that it didn't matter anymore.

If you want to begin this process, look for at least one good thing about the person who offended you. Too often we see only bad things in others, but you can almost always find something good in your offender if you'll look for it.

When I saw Leroy Jackson in that hotel, I remembered one good thing about him. When we were in the Job Corps together, he was the only one in camp who owned a car. Sometimes he would give me a ride off base so I could buy a pastrami sandwich. That was the only good thing I could think about him, but I let that one positive thought personify our whole relationship. When I embraced him in the lobby, I hugged that pastrami sandwich!

I COULDN'T FORGIVE MY ENEMIES BEFORE I MET GOD.

Stop replaying the hurt in your memory. Quit holding on to it. The longer you carry a grudge, the heavier it gets. Release your enemies out of the jailhouse that's inside your mind. If you don't, you'll keep thinking about what they did. But if you'll use the key of forgiveness to unlock the jailhouse doors, you'll discover—as I did—that you not only set your offenders free, but set yourself free as well.

TIPS FROM GEORGE'S CORNER
ON FORGIVING OTHERS

- View your enemy through the eyes of compassion and pity.
- Find and focus on at least one good thing about your enemy.
- Look for a bigger issue than the one you're upset about.
- Release your enemies out of the jailhouse inside your mind.

4
WHAT WILL PEOPLE THINK OF ME?

Isn't it strange how fear works? Some people are terrified to fly on a plane, while others love it. Although many people are afraid to be punched, I wasn't afraid to step into the ring to fight some of the toughest boxers in the world—Muhammad Ali, Joe Frazier, Ken Norton, and others.

Me? Like so many people, I feared being rejected by others. I wanted to be loved and accepted by everyone. But after my conversion, I discovered that unanimous approval was never going to happen. Friends started avoiding me. Even my family didn't understand what had happened to me. They all thought I had flipped out.

And I can't say that I blame them. I had felt the same way about church people most of my life. I didn't want anything to do with them—and now that I was following Jesus, not many of my former friends wanted to be around me either!

I knew well that bitter taste of rejection when I lost my heavyweight boxing title to Muhammad Ali. Everyone loves a winner, but few reporters want to interview the person who loses. My friends in Hollywood stopped calling me. When I was champion, Bob Hope called me to be on his shows. After I lost to Ali, he never called again. One rejection after another seemed to have a domino effect. Fewer people were asking for my autograph. The sports magazines wanted pictures of Ali instead of me. In the world of sports, sometimes you're only as popular as your last victory.

But now I was feeling a different kind of rejection. Not because I lost a fight, but because I had committed my life to God and had changed my ways. I was a completely different person than the old George, and my acquaintances had a hard time knowing how to react to me. I also struggled with making adjustments in my relationships. How do you tell someone that you "don't do that anymore" without feeling some tension?

If you're like me, you don't want to be snubbed. You want everyone to love and embrace you. But ultimately your belief in God will meet resistance, which forces you to either shut up or speak up. I eventually discovered that it was more important for me to tell the truth, even at the risk of being shunned. I had to get over my fear of other people's opinions of me because sharing my testimony was more important to me—and apparently more important to God. But learning how to tell the public what had happened to me wasn't easy.

TELLING MY STORY IN PUBLIC

About a month after my conversion, I called Dr. Robert Schuller, the senior pastor of a large church in Garden Grove, California, which is now known as the Crystal Cathedral. I had spoken at his church two years prior to this, *before* I became a believer. After I lost my fight to Muhammad Ali, my advisers told me that I needed to clean up my "bad guy" image. Ali had a large group of fans, they said, and someone told me I could probably gather a respectable following if I started speaking in churches. Dr. Schuller invited me to speak at a prayer group.

Since I had never spoken in a church before, I didn't even know where to begin.

"What do I talk about?" I asked.

"Well, George," Dr. Schuller replied, "Muhammad Ali is always talking about Allah, so why don't you talk about Jesus?"

"Okay," I said. "No problem."

Even though I wasn't a believer at the time, I stood before the crowd and gave my little talk about Jesus. Ali's followers would always chant, "Ali! Ali!" I was hoping that this bunch would jump up and yell, "Foreman! Foreman! Foreman!"

They didn't.

They applauded my speech, but that was about it. When no massive following materialized, my speaking tour of churches fizzled out. *What a bunch of losers,* I thought. *I'm not going to waste any more of my time with them.* I was done speaking to the church crowd. Associating with them didn't help reform my image one bit.

But after my encounter with God in the dressing room, I now had a genuine spiritual experience to share. I called Dr. Schuller and told him about what happened to me after the Jimmy Young fight.

> IN THE WORLD OF SPORTS, YOU'RE ONLY AS POPULAR AS YOUR LAST WIN.

"Dr. Schuller," I explained, "I'm not lying to you—it really happened. I was just pretending when I spoke at your church before, but I'm not joking this time. I'm telling you the truth; *He's alive!*"

"Well, George," he replied in his deep, resonating voice. "I'm a psychologist and an ordained minister, and I believe you."

I wasn't sure if he was merely being polite, so again I said, "Dr. Schuller, I'm not kidding you. What happened to me was real."

He assured me again, "I believe you, George."

"I'm not lying, Dr. Schuller."

"George," he firmly asserted, "I believe you! Please do me a favor. Come and share this with my congregation. Tell them what happened to you."

I flew back to California a different man than two years earlier when I had spoken at the church. This time I stood before the congregation of three thousand people and shared about my death experience in the dressing room, going to that horrible dark place, seeing the blood on my hands—the whole story.

Dr. Schuller's church was the first public place where I shared my testimony. But for some reason, I thought my sermon would be confidential—that I was just speaking to *that* congregation. With my newfound faith, I was still somewhat unsure about how to tell others what I had discovered, and I was selective concerning who would hear about my experience. Little did I realize that the entire country would soon be watching it on television.

ALL THOSE NEGATIVE REACTIONS HAD PROGRAMMED ME TO BELIEVE THAT "THOSE RELIGIOUS FOLKS" WERE WEIRD.

About two weeks after I spoke in Dr. Schuller's beautiful Garden Grove, California, church, I opened the newspaper in Houston and noticed an ad for Dr. Schuller's television show, *The Hour of Power*. I was stunned to find out they were going to broadcast my testimony nationwide!

I wasn't ready for that much publicity about my faith. An experience like mine can bring applause, but it can also draw a lot of ridicule. In spite of what God had done for me, I didn't want people making fun of me, and I had no desire to be fodder for some late-night comedian's routine.

PROGRAMMED FOR EMBARRASSMENT

After seeing that ad in the paper, two incidents from my past immediately popped into my mind. First, I recalled a time when some of my girlfriends had come to see me box in Canada. One of the girls mentioned casually that she had recently talked with a star baseball player for the Los Angeles Dodgers.

"Guess what he told me?" she asked, rolling her eyes. "He said he's been *born again*."

The other young woman started laughing and replied, "You'd better get out of my face with that junk!"

I took careful stock of what the women were saying. Before the ballplayer found religion, they had admired the guy. Now they were making fun of him. I knew which side of that issue I wanted to be on.

"Yeah, he's stupid," I agreed. "He's probably crazy, too," I added. I didn't want anyone to ever ridicule me for being religious the way they had that well-known major league baseball player.

The second eye-opener came after my sisters had gone to an Al Green concert. Upon returning home, one sister said, "We went to hear Al Green tonight, and the music was great. But then he got up and started talking about God." In disgust she placed her hands on her hips and snapped, "I didn't go to that concert to hear a sermon! I go to church when I want to hear a sermon."

My former girlfriends and my sisters weren't the only ones who poked fun at religious people. Many of my friends did the same thing. After I was born again, I was embarrassed to tell them because I didn't want them to laugh at me. I didn't want to be the butt of their jokes.

Just after my conversion, one of the first people I told about what had happened to me was my sister, Gloria. Being cautious about who heard my testimony, I instructed her not to tell anyone. Even though my sister believed my story, it didn't make sense to her. She said, "Yeah, George, your experience sounds like the book of Revelation. You need to read it." I had never heard of the book of Revelation, but I decided to read it someday soon.

Although I didn't realize it at the time, all those negative reactions had programmed me to believe that "those religious folks" were weird. I didn't want anyone to believe I was that way. Everyone I knew made fun of people who went to church, especially joking about the hypocrites, the ones who didn't live what they claimed to believe. Even after my dynamic conversion experience, that warped concept still had a firm grip on my mind. I believed in Christ, but I didn't want to be labeled as a religious nut or called weird because of my newfound faith.

Now, thanks to Dr. Schuller, my testimony was going to be broadcast across the nation on television. I wasn't ready for any more ridicule, so I went into seclusion. I didn't go to the barber shop because they were saying, "George is talking about God. Jimmy Young beat him, and he's trying to come up with an excuse about God." I heard those kinds of remarks everywhere in town. I didn't want everybody laughing at me, like those girls poking fun at that baseball player. Because I couldn't stand the thought of being seen in front of the camera and then ridiculed, I resigned my television contract as a boxing commentator working with Howard Cosell. I never wanted to be seen in public again.

REPROGRAMMING MY MIND

I was in total confusion about what to do with my life. I decided I would stay at my mom's house and wait for further instructions from God. My sister Gloria knew that I needed guidance, so she brought a preacher to the house to talk with me. I told him about dying and seeing the blood on my hands, but now I was confused about what it all meant.

The preacher nodded his head in understanding as he listened to me. Then, opening his Bible, he read to me about a man named Cornelius having a vision and seeing an angel. The angel told Cornelius, "Your prayers and your alms have come up for a memorial before God."[1]

I perked up. "That's in the Bible?" Even though I had seen a vision, I didn't know that other people had experienced something similar.

He said, "Yep."

The preacher went on to explain that a man named Peter had a vision of animals in a sheet coming down from heaven. A voice said, "Peter, kill and eat."

"That's in the Bible, too?" I asked.

Again he said, "Yep."

"How long has that been in the Bible?" I asked. "Do you mean to tell me that other people have seen things like I saw?" I had heard that Jesus Christ had done miracles, but I didn't know other people in the Bible had miraculous things happen to them.

"Some people have seen a lot more than that," the preacher said with a grin.

Suddenly, I didn't feel so isolated regarding what had happened to me in Puerto Rico. I thought I was the only one in the world who had experienced such an unusual vision. I asked the preacher to read the Scripture to me again, so he did. Then I had him read it again.

I was genuinely relieved to know that unusual experiences similar to mine had happened to people in the Bible. I laughed and said, "Man! I guess I'm not so crazy after all!"

Even then, I thought the church world wasn't ready to hear what I had to say. I attended a small church for six months before I ever told my testimony. When I finally did tell my story, when I came to the part where I yelled in the dressing room, "Jesus Christ is coming alive in me!" everyone in the congregation cheered and applauded. That helped me overcome a lot of my doubts and fears about sharing my testimony. From that point on, I started telling everyone I could.

WHY DID GOD CHOOSE ME?

Many times I've asked God, *Why me? Why did you choose me to have this experience? I was just a bad boy who didn't know anything.* But God always has a reason for the things He does.

I believe one reason He picked me for that experience was because I held the world's heavyweight boxing title, which opened doors to meet numerous celebrities and world leaders. Maybe God chose me because He wanted to use me to speak to them. Perhaps that's why He gave me that strange "virtual-reality tour" of those celebrities' lives while I was in the dressing room.

During my boxing career, I met numerous entertainers such as Harry Bellefonte, Sammy Davis Jr., and so many others; I was honored to meet famous politicians and national leaders such as President Lyndon Johnson and President Bill Clinton; and, of course, I came to know a host of famous athletes. In spite of their fortune and fame, most of these celebrities seemed unfulfilled. So after I truly became a changed man, I tried to share my testimony with every one of them when I had the opportunity.

Although they had all accomplished great things, none of them ever claimed to have had a divine encounter. Not a single one of them could say, "George, I was in my dressing room one day, and I saw blood on my hands and head, and I cried out, 'Jesus Christ is coming alive in me!' And then I walked away from everything I had and gave my life to God. I could have been dead in my grave and lost my soul, but now I know that Jesus is alive!" I have yet to meet anyone who has told me that.

Whenever I tell my story, I'm often met with skepticism. If someone raises an eyebrow and gives me that "I don't believe you" look, I just quit talking. If they aren't willing to listen, it does no good to continue. But if they're interested in what I have to say, I'll keep sharing my entire story with them.

When I began reading the Bible, I discovered that the apostle Paul kept telling others about his remarkable conversion experience on the road to Damascus, where a light brighter than the sun shone around him and a voice from heaven spoke to him. When Paul stood on trial before King Agrippa, he described every detail of his testimony. Agrippa must have been impressed with Paul's story because the king told him, "Paul, you almost persuade me to be a Christian." That same reaction was how many responded to me—*almost* persuaded. Many of the people I told didn't want to believe me because they thought they had too much to lose.

> I CAN UNDERSTAND WHY THEY MIGHT BE SUSPICIOUS WHEN THEY HEAR MY STORY . . . BUT IT DID HAPPEN TO ME.

I can understand why they might be suspicious when they hear my story. I would be skeptical, too. If someone had told me that he or she had died, come back to life, had a vision, and started quoting Scriptures without having learned them, I wouldn't have believed it either! Because it sounds so outlandish, I can understand why they may be reluctant to believe me. But it did happen to me, and just because they don't believe it doesn't change what happened to me.

Now, it doesn't matter what anyone says about me; I know what God says is true. And that has been the key to overcoming my fear of other people's opinions—letting the truth be my guide. I had to reprogram my mind by replacing false ideas with true ones.

Finding Jesus Christ was the best thing that ever happened to me, and my life gets better every day. I'm not going to let anything destroy my testimony and the great relationship with God that I have experienced. I will keep telling my story until I'm unable to say it anymore.

After I overcame my fear of rejection, I called those two girls who made fun of the baseball player and told them what had happened to me. I was surprised when one girl said, "I've been trying to get my life together, and that's what I needed to hear." It was like she was thinking, *If George can change, maybe I can change, too.* Now they had heard about being born again from a professional baseball player and a professional boxer. And they knew what I was like before my conversion, so they had plenty of reasons to believe that God could change them, too.

I called the great boxer Archie Moore and told him my story. He said, "I believe you. Maybe I need to get closer to God myself." It was like everyone was waiting on me to pave the way so they could find God, too.

For several weeks, I spent entire days and nights looking up people's phone numbers and making telephone calls. I called Muhammad Ali, Jimmy Young, and Joe Frazier, telling each of them about my conversion. Then I called my friend Sammy Davis Jr. when he was performing in Australia and explained that I had met God. He was one of the people I had seen in that virtual-reality vision. I told him that Jesus Christ could really help him.

"Really?" Sammy replied.

I said, "Yeah, you need to give Jesus a chance."

After talking for a while, he cut me off. "That's really nice, George. Well, I need to go now."

Not long after that phone call, Sammy died. I don't know if he ever trusted Jesus with his life, but I know I pointed him in the right direction. That's all I could do, and that's all God asks us to do—lift up Jesus and point people to Him.

Another time I received a phone call, and a strange sounding voice on the other end said, "I need to talk to Mr. George Foreman." I thought someone was trying to pull a trick on me, disguising his voice like a reporter wanting to interview me.

"Who?" I asked, trying to identify the voice.

"I need to talk with Mr. George Foreman."

I wondered how the caller got my telephone number. "Who is this?" I demanded to know.

He burst out laughing. "This is Marvin Gaye, George."

"Marvin! How are you doing?" After the great singer and I talked for a while, I worked the conversation around to my dressing room experience. I told Marvin that I had died, gone to the other side, had come back into my body, and seen the blood where Jesus had been crucified. I explained that I had found Jesus Christ, and I described the difference He had made in my life.

"Marvin," I pleaded, "maybe it's time for you to get straight."

"Why me, George?" he asked, as if offended. "Why are you messing with me?"

After that, he didn't want to talk to me anymore. It wasn't but a year later that Marvin passed away, too.

These were *great* people, but no one was calling me, wanting to know how to find God. So I contacted them to tell them my story. It's sad, but most of them didn't want to hear the truth. They would change the subject or say, "That's nice for you, George."

Today I travel everywhere, telling everyone who will listen. I'm grateful for God saving me. People who are not celebrities—common folks—want to hear my testimony more than the rich and famous people do. I'm convinced that God gives all of us a chance to know Him. He gives us the opportunity, and if we'll say yes to Him, He will choose us. But He won't force Himself on anyone.

OVERCOMING EVIL WITH GOOD

After I retired from boxing, not everyone liked my decision. Once, I went to San Francisco, where one of my friends contacted me saying that his brother—a highly intelligent man—needed to talk with me about an urgent matter. I assumed he was going through a difficult time and possibly needed my help. I agreed to contact him and schedule a time to connect.

Calling him on the telephone, I introduced myself and asked what I could do for him.

"Hi, George," he said. "I heard about you finding God. Listen, I'm glad you called me, because I have something important to tell you. Do you know what you need to do?"

"What?"

"You should go to the Golden Gate Bridge," he said matter-of-factly, "walk to the middle of the bridge, and jump off!"

I couldn't believe my ears and was taken aback by his dislike for me. People had told me to do lots of things before, but jumping off the Golden Gate Bridge was a first!

He wasn't through, so he continued his verbal assault. "Do you know what you had? You took that incredible boxing career, threw it out the window, and just walked away from all that money you could have made. When minorities have an opportunity like you had, they should never let it go." He told me that I was a fool for believing that serving the Lord was more important than making money.

The hostile voice continued, "Now, you just get going—and go jump off that bridge!"

Perhaps the man was testing me to see if I had really changed. The old George would have tracked him down and sent him to the canvas, but the new George knew he was a lost soul. I had taken time out of my schedule to talk with him, by his request, and belittling me was his "urgent matter." But he made me realize that many others were probably thinking the same thing about me.

I wanted him to become a better man than the one who had just talked to me. I wasn't going to allow his hatred to get to me, so I returned kindness to him instead. I invited him to contact me if he ever needed to talk.

"Stay in touch with me, okay?" I said as I prepared to hang up the phone.

"Yeah," he spat out, "I'll stay in touch with you, you blankety-blank. . . ." He was still cussing me out as I put down the receiver.

Although many people were thrilled that I had found the Lord, others didn't like me because of it. I wasn't surprised when I lost some friends. I'd call them and leave messages, but they wouldn't return my calls. They didn't want to talk to me. But that's okay. I knew I had a Friend who will never forsake me and always return my calls.

Perhaps you're intimidated by others' opinions of you. As you've just read, you're not the only one. I had to conquer this giant myself.

So how can you overcome the craving for people's approval? The answer is actually pretty simple. The truth will set you free. Your desire to please God must be greater than your urge to make others happy. You must find your acceptance in God, not in other people.

God accepts you and forgives you the moment you trust Him with your life. He'll give you the inner strength to live right and to do the right thing, even when other people laugh at you or get angry with you. Putting His strength into practice in your life is your decision.

TIPS FROM GEORGE'S CORNER
ON OVERCOMING REJECTION

- Believe what God says about you instead of what people say.
- Please God first and people second.
- When someone says something hateful to you, respond kindly with a nice comment.

5 A FIGHTING PREACHER

AFTER I FOUND JESUS CHRIST, I HAD NO IDEA I WOULD BECOME A pastor and an evangelist one day. I've had no formal Bible training, no college or seminary training, but God placed a call on my life.

About a month after my conversion, when Dr. Robert Schuller invited me to his church in California to give my testimony, I noticed Dr. Schuller's son reading his Bible. I looked over his shoulder and read: "If then you were raised with Christ, seek those things which are above, where Christ is, sitting at the right hand of God."[1]

Those words seemed to leap off the pages as if speaking right to me. "Let me see that," I said to him. "That's the way I feel! Will you write that down for me?" Being a new believer, I didn't even know if that verse was in the Old or New Testament, but I wanted to remember it. When I went back to my hotel, I asked a friend if he would buy a Bible for me.

"Sure," he answered. "What kind?"

"I don't know. The same kind your mother has, I guess."

He called his mother in Alabama and found out she had a King James

Version. He ran out, bought a Bible, and brought it back to me. The first Scripture that I looked for was that verse in Colossians: "If then you were raised with Christ, seek those things which are above, where Christ is, sitting at the right hand of God."

I read it again and again. "That's the way I feel—risen with Christ!"

That was how I first learned to read the Bible, one verse at a time. Then I started reading entire passages, and before long, I was so fascinated with God's Word, I had a hard time putting the book down. Next, I needed to find a church back home, where I could learn more about God.

BECOMING A PART OF THE LOCAL FAMILY OF GOD

Shortly after returning to Houston, I heard about a church named the Church of the Lord Jesus Christ. As I searched for the address, I drove up and down the street, looking for a large cathedral. There was no cathedral to be found in that part of Houston. The church turned out to be in a small building, similar to a convenience store. I drove up in my expensive Stutz Blackhawk automobile with a wire wheel mounted on the back and climbed out wearing my immaculate, red suit. I slipped in the door and sat on the back row, thinking no one would see me. (Of course, with my fancy car and flashy clothes, how could the worshipers in that church *not* notice me?)

At the end of the preacher's sermon, he invited people to come to the front of the church to pray. A number of members of the congregation got up from their seats, walked to the front, and got on their knees. I decided to do the same. I fell to my knees and confessed to God all of my sins, doubts, and fears. I figured that I had been living on borrowed time and expected to die at any moment. As I continued to pray that evening, the feeling of ecstasy that I had experienced in the Puerto Rican dressing room returned to me. God refreshed me with another touch, which made me want to come back again.

The next week, I returned to the church. After the sermon, I walked to the front and fell on my knees, hoping to feel those same sensations that I'd felt previously. This time, however, I didn't feel anything. Even though I didn't experience a thrill like I had on my first visit, I continued attending the church to hear the sermons. After about three months, someone invited me to attend the Sunday morning services. I didn't know they had morning services, too. I thought this was only a night church!

It took six months of attending before I worked up the courage to give my testimony in front of the congregation. I hadn't spoken in a church since being at Dr. Schuller's, because from time to time, I still battled the fear of what people thought about me. I didn't want people to think I was crazy. However, my fears quickly vanished as I began to share my experience with the audience.

> **AS I CONTINUED TO PRAY, THE FEELING OF ECSTASY THAT I HAD EXPERIENCED IN THE PUERTO RICAN DRESSING ROOM RETURNED TO ME.**

When I told them about being in the dressing room and shouting, "Jesus Christ is coming alive in me!" the entire congregation erupted into applause and cheering.

FASTING FOR TWENTY-ONE DAYS

Not long after I gave my testimony at the church, I went to visit my aunt in Houston. While staying there, I had a dream in which I saw a large, open book. Every line that filled the pages repeated the same phrase: "Evangelistic 21." I had never heard the word "evangelistic" before, so I didn't understand what it meant.

I asked my aunt if she understood the meaning of the dream. She replied, "Maybe God is trying to tell you something."

I went to my preacher friend, Brother Masters, to see if he could interpret my dream.

"Twenty-one is the number of a fast," he explained. "God is calling you to be an evangelist, and you need to fast for twenty-one days. You're not supposed to eat any food for three weeks."

"Twenty-one days without food? That's impossible!"

"Well, I once fasted for forty days, like Jesus and Moses did," he replied. "It won't be easy, but you can do it. You do need to drink a lot of water, though."

I figured if God wanted me to go without eating that long, He would have to help me do it. "Okay," I said. "I'm going to do it. I'll fast for twenty-one days and nights."

It was tough at first, going without food, avoiding those delicious goodies my mother knew how to make. After the first week, I got scared because my physical system seemed to be changing. I didn't need to go to the bathroom after the fourth day. By the eleventh day, I had lost over twenty pounds. I hadn't eaten any food, but I did drink water. My mother thought I was crazy and fretted that I would starve myself to death.

On the fourteenth day of fasting, God started revealing truths to me as I read the Bible. It was as if He shone a light on certain verses that I needed to understand. By the seventeenth day, I started noticing every billboard that advertised food. I knew the location of every restaurant, fast-food drive-thru, grocery store, and daily special in town. Everywhere I drove, the golden arches seemed to multiply. I was so hungry that I was ready to eat almost anything—or everything!

By the twenty-first day, I had lost approximately forty pounds. The morning after my fast ended, I ate a large breakfast and drank a gallon of milk, which gave me hiccups for several days. I had never been so thankful for food in all my life!

So what good came out of it? The fast focused my attention on God and His Word (after I stopped thinking about how hungry I was, that is); it allowed me to review and relive some of my negative experiences and purged some bad memories out of me. But more than anything, I developed an incredible appetite to read God's Word and grow closer to the Lord. For the next two years, I spent several hours every day studying the Bible, along with commentaries, Bible dictionaries, and other reference books.

Although some people probably thought my religious experience wouldn't last, I was serious about living for God. My friends and family members understood that I was serious after that fast. They knew I loved to eat, and I couldn't and wouldn't give up food for that long without divine help.

God honored my fast in another way that I wasn't expecting. He would soon be flinging open many doors to use my gift of evangelism. But first I had to learn how to preach.

FROM PREACHING ON THE STREETS
TO AROUND THE WORLD

One day after I had spoken at my church, a young teenager named Dexter Wilson approached me. "George, you like to tell your story so much, why don't we go out together on the streets and preach?"

"Preach on the street corners?" I asked. I'd never heard of that.

"Yeah, I've seen 'em do it before."

Although Dexter was just a teenager, he taught me how to street preach. We purchased an amplifier and microphone and drove to Shreveport, Louisiana. We set up our sound system near some apartment buildings, and Dexter started speaking into his handheld mic: "Well, praise the Lord, brothers and sisters. I'm not here to lift up myself. I'm here to lift up Jesus. . . ."

After he preached for a little while, it was my turn. Dexter wasn't scared, but I was! My palms were sweaty from being so nervous. I had no idea what I would say when he handed me the microphone.

My mind went blank, so I just repeated what Dexter had said. "Well, praise the Lord, brothers and sisters. I'm not here to lift up myself. I'm here to lift up Jesus."

"OKAY, I'M GOING TO DO IT. I'LL FAST FOR TWENTY-ONE DAYS AND NIGHTS."

No one knew who I was. I was wearing overalls and a flannel shirt and didn't look like the George Foreman they had seen on television. Dexter tried to get me to identify myself, but I resisted at first. But when I saw that people were just walking by and ignoring me, I decided to go ahead and tell them who I was.

As people walked by, I announced, "Yeah, folks, this is George Foreman talking. That's right, I'm the former heavyweight champion of the world. I'm the one who fought the great Muhammad Ali."

Immediately people stopped and a crowd gathered. I noticed people pointing at me and telling others. I overheard someone say, "Hey, that's George Foreman. He beat Joe Frazier."

Now that I had people's attention, I continued my sermon. "Yes, God saved me, George Foreman. I was lost in sin, but now I'm saved . . ."

From Shreveport, we moved on to Tyler, Texas, where we continued preaching on the streets. Dexter and I preached in several cities in Texas and Louisiana. We even preached in Los Angeles. All I had to say was, "Yes, folks, this is George Foreman . . ." and people would gather to listen.

News spread about my conversion, and soon I received invitations from all over the country to give my testimony. God opened doors for me to speak in a number of schools and colleges in California. I traveled all over Canada, speaking in churches from small to large. Several producers of television programs invited me to share about my conversion to Christianity, which I gladly did.

> **WHEN I SPOKE AT SAN QUENTIN, SOME OF THE MOST HARDENED CRIMINALS GAVE THEIR LIVES TO THE LORD.**

I traveled back to Zaire, Africa, on an evangelical mission and gave my testimony before sixty thousand people in the same arena where I fought Muhammad Ali. Because so many remembered the famous boxing match, people came from everywhere, wanting to hear what I had to say. Nearly everyone in Africa had pulled for Ali to beat me. But on this visit, they were excited to see me.

Wherever I went in Africa, people pointed at me and said, "That's him! That's him!" God used my fame to get their attention so I could preach His Word to them. I was so glad to return to Zaire a different man than the first time I was there.

ORDAINED TO PREACH

Even though I had done a lot of preaching, I was not yet an ordained minister. One day I received an urgent request to visit a hospital in Houston to pray for a boy in critical condition. The young man had been shot four times and was hanging on for dear life. Upon arriving at the hospital, I was turned away because their policy only permitted ordained ministers to visit patients in the intensive care unit.

Up until then, I had ministered as a layperson without any problem. Now I realized I couldn't get into hospitals and prisons without being ordained. I didn't want to run into any more obstacles that prevented me from ministering to people. Soon after this, the Church of the Lord Jesus

Christ ordained me as an evangelist so I could continue to carry out my ministry. My ordination allowed me to visit hospitals and prisons to share my testimony.

The Lord opened doors for me to speak in a number of prisons. When I spoke at San Quentin, some of their most hardened criminals responded to my testimony and gave their lives to the Lord. Afterward, they formed a long line so I could baptize them in a large tub.

I've had a passion to visit prisons so I could preach to the inmates, and I've enjoyed doing that. But I've concluded that the guards, counselors, and other officials need as much encouragement as the men and women who are incarcerated. They work in one of the toughest environments imaginable, which can be extremely degrading and discouraging. Sometimes they will release a prisoner whom they believe has been reformed only to see him return to the penitentiary a few years later. So when I visit prisons, I minister to the employees as well as the inmates.

The greatest thrill of my life is to see lives changed. If God can change a hardened person like I used to be, He can do it for anyone. That's what I believe and that's what I preach.

PASTOR OF A SMALL CHURCH

Reality punctured my idealistic ideas about the Christian life when my pastor and spiritual mentor became involved in what we sometimes call "moral indiscretions"—a nice way of saying the person committed adultery. I was sorely disappointed that a man I had loved and respected so much could be unfaithful to his wife and children, but I was even more disheartened when I discovered that many in the church condoned the pastor's actions and made excuses for his conduct. When I publicly voiced my opinion regarding the matter, I soon found myself in the minority and was asked to leave the church.

I felt betrayed and hurt, but it was a good lesson: I realized that I had to keep my eyes on Jesus, not just someone who claims to believe in Him. I had been preaching occasionally in the church, and I loved to preach, so I bought thirty minutes of radio time on a Houston station and continued preaching. On my show, I talked a little about boxing and a lot about the good Lord. I was living in Humble, a suburb of Houston, so when I went into the city to do my radio show, it wasn't unusual for several friends from my former church to ask me to lead a Bible study or to pray with them. Three or four of us met in various homes; soon there were six or eight, then ten people attending.

Before long, someone asked, "George, do you think we could have a service in my home?"

"I guess so. Why not? The early church met in people's homes. I guess we can too." We began meeting informally at various homes in Houston, and before long, the crowds became too large for most houses to accommodate. Eventually, we bought a piece of land and an old, dilapidated building on the northeast side of Houston. I owned a large tent that I had intended to use in holding outdoor "evangelistic" or "revival" services, so we put up the tent in the lot next to the building and held services there while we renovated the old structure. I didn't really intend to start a new church, but eventually we found it beneficial to organize.

I've been serving as the pastor of the Church of the Lord Jesus Christ in Houston since 1980. Even though I've spoken as an evangelist to huge crowds all over the world, only fifty or sixty people attend my church on any given Sunday. It's a mystery to me why the church remains small.

Our church seats about two hundred people, and it is rarely full. But if I'm asked to speak at a motivational seminar, people will come from everywhere to hear me. Multitudes of people paid $50 or $100 to see me box on pay-per-view, but in my church we might have three or four visitors on Sunday morning, and it's free. Maybe people find boxing more interesting than God's Word because they don't realize which of the two will last forever. Regardless, I don't let the size of the crowd affect whether or not I will give my best effort. The Lord prepared me in advance for my simple ministry.

At the end of 1978, a guest minister spoke in our church for several nights. I put on my overalls and a plaid shirt and went to hear him. As he was preaching, he pointed to me and said, "Stand up, young man."

I stood up.

"Do you see those overalls you have on?"

"Yes, sir," I replied.

"Do you see that plaid shirt?"

"Yeah."

"The Lord wants you to know that's a picture of the ministry you're going to have. It's going to be a very simple ministry. It's going to be just like your clothes—very plain."

A simple ministry? That didn't make any sense to me whatsoever. I was well-known even then, because I had already been an Olympic gold medalist and the heavyweight boxing champion of the world. And now he was telling me I was just going to have a simple little ministry like the overalls I was wearing?

Nevertheless, that preacher's prophetic words have proven to be true. My ministry over the years has been just like he described—a simple message to the common person. I believe God uses the small crowd at church to help keep me humble. But I have found that it's not the size of the church that impresses God. It's the size of a person's heart.

TIPS FROM GEORGE'S CORNER ON MINISTRY

- Faithfully serve in the ministry that you've received from God.
- Use your spiritual gift to build up and strengthen your church.
- Be concerned about pleasing God and not how many people notice you serving.

6
BEING OPTIMISTIC IN A PESSIMISTIC WORLD

As I WAS GROWING UP, ONE OF THE OFTEN-REPEATED PHRASES I heard from my mother was, "Oh Lord" this or "Oh Lord" that. My mom lived with constant stress and strain, working night and day to take care of our family.

I frequently said to myself, *One day I'm going to be rich, and I'm going to make enough money that Mom will never have to have to say, "Oh, Lord, this or that" anymore.* I had big dreams and plans. Unfortunately, my plans didn't include school.

School and I just didn't get along. It didn't matter which one I attended— and I attended several before I became a teenager—I failed nearly every class. After a while, I decided that school was not the place I wanted to be. I could smell mathematics from miles away, and I did my best to avoid anything that hinted at science or history. I hated school, and couldn't see any reason why I needed to be there all day. I just couldn't convince my mom of that fact.

Instead, I became an expert hooky-player. I headed off to school each morning, just like my siblings, but somehow or other I never quite arrived at class. I waited long enough to be sure that Mom had gone to work, then I made my way full circle back home. Knowing the doors would be locked, I left a window unlocked each morning. I crawled through the window, climbed back into bed, and went back to sleep.

YOUR ATTITUDE TOWARD YOUR CIRCUMSTANCES DETERMINES YOUR HAPPINESS.

Later in the afternoon, I made sure that I got back to school before the dismissal time, to give the appearance that I was coming out of school along with all my other friends and family members.

My plan was working well until one day when I was sneaking through the window, and my cousin Rita caught me. Rita had been staying with my family while she was searching for a job, and she normally was not at home during the day. When she saw me climb through the window, she shouted, "George! What in the world are you doing?"

I was just as surprised to see her as she was me, so I immediately began stammering, trying to come up with an instant excuse for climbing through the window when I was supposed to be at school.

"Oh, oh! Hi, Rita. I didn't know you were here, or I would have come through the front door. I forgot something . . . and had to come home from school to find it."

Rita stood with her hands on her hips, looking at me as though to say, "George Foreman, you aren't fooling anyone." After a few moments, she said, "Come on in and go to sleep, George. Don't worry, I won't tell anyone."

"I told you that I forgot something."

"You know that you weren't going to school," Rita said.

"Oh yes, I was!"

"George, go to sleep. Nobody in this family is ever going to amount to anything. Not your brothers or sisters, not me, and not you, either. Go back to sleep."

I got so upset with Rita for spouting all her dire predictions of failure on our family that I stomped out of the bedroom and slammed the front door on my way out of the house. I was so mad I almost went back to school!

I couldn't believe that Rita was giving up on me and writing me off without even a fight. Over the years, Rita's words haunted me, but they also drove me. I was determined to make something of my life and to make every day count.

When I finally won the world heavyweight boxing title, Rita was right there, saying, "I always knew you could do it, George!"

I don't blame Rita, though, for not believing in me back when we were younger. The truth is, my relationship with God is the reason I have such a positive outlook on life. Before I found Christ, I was blind. I was like a man wandering across a desert with sand blowing in my eyes. I couldn't see anything. But when Jesus came into my life, He opened my eyes and started showing me all the good things that I couldn't see previously. God changed my heart and altered the way I view everything.

Granted, it is possible to think positively without having Jesus in your heart. But without Him, you'll never have His lasting perspective on the issues you're dealing with or going through. For those who love Him, He has promised to make something good out of everything that happens to us. That right there is the reason I can have a positive attitude in every situation.

Ever since I got my wake-up call, I have been an eternal optimist. When something bad happens to me, I just remember that dark pit—and immediately I realize how good I have it! The worst day on Earth is far better than being in that place. No matter how dark the clouds, I look for a ray of sunshine in every circumstance.

People who are around me can feel my happiness. When I talk about how I enjoy living, it's not like I'm giving them a lecture. It's real. Some days when I get excited, my kids will say, "Get real, Dad."

I tell them, "This is real! Life is a privilege." I'll admit that being an optimist in a world full of pessimists isn't easy. But it sure is fun!

I'm convinced that my attitude has everything to do with my happiness. It's not our circumstances that determine our happiness, but our attitudes *toward* our circumstances. Pessimists only see the bad things going on, never the good. When they look at a rosebush, they see thorns instead of flowers. They complain about what they don't have while ignoring what they do have. They emphasize what they've lost rather than focusing on what they have left. They are constantly talking about what they *can't* do instead of what they *can* do. That's why they're always upset and never happy.

ACCENTUATE THE POSITIVE

An old song says, "You've got to accentuate the positive and eliminate the negative." That's the key to having a good relationship with someone. Whenever I look at others, I accentuate the positive in them and eliminate the negative. I concentrate on all their good points and overlook their flaws. That's why I can have good feelings even about my enemies and no longer hate them. It doesn't matter who it is—you can usually find some little reason to say, "I love him for *that*."

The secret to having a positive attitude is the same as the secret to having good relationships: accentuate the positive and eliminate the negative. Just as I look for the best in others, I've also learned to search for the best in my circumstances. No matter what happens, I choose to focus on the positive rather than the negative.

> **THAT LITTLE BIT OF HAPPINESS HAS TO BECOME BIGGER IN MY MIND THAN THE PREDICAMENT I'M IN.**

I've disciplined my mind so I don't even allow negative thoughts to penetrate. If I have any unusual gifts at all, I have a gift that helps me not to hear anything negative. For instance, if my trainer said to me, "George, your left jab is too slow," I couldn't hear that. Of course, I could hear it with my ears, but my heart and mind refused to allow that statement to land. But if my trainer came to me and said, "George, I can show you how you can make your left jab faster," I could hear that! "Show me how to do that." I can always hear the positive statement, but I've trained my mind to reject the negative.

Life is never so bad that I can't find something to smile about. It doesn't take any effort at all to think negatively. It almost seems to come naturally. Instead of dwelling on thoughts that make me miserable, I choose to think thoughts that make me happy. It won't happen automatically, so I make an effort to have a positive attitude. I look for something in every situation that brings me a little bit of happiness. After I've found that thing that makes me happy, it then has to become bigger in my mind than the predicament I'm in. When I look at my circumstances in this way, the positive overrules the negative.

I'm not talking about denying reality or living in an imaginary world where only good things happen. No, I'm talking about living in this real world, but finding the good side of it. Every situation contains a mixture of good and bad. Just as a battery has a positive and a negative terminal, every situation has a plus and a minus side. I get to decide which part I'll concentrate on. I can choose whether I'll give my attention to the plus side or the minus side. What I focus on and think about will determine the attitude I'll have in that situation.

Every day, whether you realize it or not, you're spying out the land where you live and where you work, looking for either the best or the worst. Your attitude at that moment will be determined by what you see. If you're only looking at problems, you'll become angry, depressed, and ungrateful. But if you'll search for and find something good in every situation, you'll discover a secret that few people know—happiness is always attached to seeing the pleasant side of circumstances.

A MISERABLE MILLIONAIRE

Before I met God, my attitude was about as bad as it could get. Even when everything was going well for me, I couldn't see it. And I didn't appreciate it. When Muhammad Ali fought me for the heavyweight championship, I received a five-million-dollar paycheck. No fighters had ever been so well-paid in the history of boxing. You'd think that being a multimillionaire would bring instant joy to my soul.

It didn't. Because I lost the boxing match, I couldn't enjoy my money. I had five million dollars in the bank but couldn't find pleasure in even one penny of it! I had such a negative attitude that I couldn't see anything good in my life. I was like the spies Moses sent into Canaan to check out the Promised Land after God's people had been miraculously delivered from Egyptian slavery. Ten out of twelve spies came back with a negative report, talking about the giants in the land, the obstacles facing them, and how they didn't have a chance. Like those pessimists, I chose to see the worst in my situation, and my stomach tied up in knots as a result. My sour attitude caused me to sink into deep depression even though I was filthy rich. Five million dollars could buy me anything I wanted—except happiness.

Every night I woke up sweating, reliving the nightmare of losing that fight to Ali. In my out-of-control imaginations, I envisioned people making fun of me behind my back. Those miserable thoughts tortured my mind for the next two and a half years, and they didn't stop until I found Christ in that dressing room. Amazingly, all those nightmares and negative thoughts ceased to haunt me. He came into my heart and brought peace to my mind.

FIVE MILLION DOLLARS COULD BUY ME ANYTHING I WANTED— EXCEPT FOR HAPPINESS.

Happiness is always a matter of the mind. It's a perspective, how I perceive everything that happens to me. I've been poor with millions of dollars. And I've been rich when I was broke. Money doesn't make me happy. It's my relationship with God that brings true happiness.

My mother was more valuable to me than a million dollars in the bank. I could do without money, but I couldn't replace my mom. I considered myself rich when my mother, aunts, and uncle were all still alive. When I was a boy, my family lived in a small, run-down, rented house. When my cousins came to see us, we all had to sleep on the floor. At dinnertime, the portions were so small that we'd sneak food from each other's plates—but we had such love for one another. That's when I was truly rich and didn't know it!

When I was seven years old, my mother was going to spank me for disobeying her. I decided to run from her to escape my punishment. I figured I could outrun her and she would never catch me.

But Mom was right behind me, yelling, "George, I'll get you!" I didn't realize she could run that fast, so I climbed a tree as high as I could. My mother started shaking that tree.

"Momma, don't do it," I pleaded. "I'm going to fall!"

"George, you come down!" She kept shaking the tree.

I was so afraid I would tumble out of that tree. "I'll die if I fall!"

"You get down right now!" she screamed as the tree continued to vibrate.

I climbed down and took my spanking, which was less painful than falling from the tree would have been.

I'm rich when I think about such memories that are dear to me. I still laugh when I think of my mom hot on my heels, running after me and shaking that tree. I cherish that memory of my mother. (I didn't then!) When I look back on my childhood, I see our pitiful little, rented house as a mansion. Even though we were poor financially, we were rich in relationships.

> **HAPPINESS IS ALWAYS A MATTER OF THE MIND.**

So if you think having lots of money makes you happy, you need to think again. Take it from someone who has been a millionaire and has also been broke. If God blesses you financially, then be thankful, help others, and spend it wisely. But remember that money doesn't make you rich. If you don't have anything more than cash in the bank, maybe you're poor after all. On the other hand, if you know the love of God and have the love of family and friends, you are rich indeed!

DON'T LET PEOPLE UPSET YOU

Sooner or later, you're going to meet some people who will upset you. They'll do things to hurt you, but don't let yourself be offended. They usually don't realize what they're doing. Just shake it off, keep a positive attitude, and move on.

I raise horses on my ranch. Sometimes when I'm trying to help them, they'll kick me or step on my toes. They don't realize that I'm the only one who will feed and take care of them. I'm the person who calls the veterinarian. One time a stallion bit me, causing a serious injury. I could have sold him after that. But I realized that the horse had no one else to take care of him.

Even though my horses are totally dependent on me, they're ignorant about how they're hurting me. So when they try to kick me, I just overlook it and keep feeding them hay. If they really understood how their actions injured me, they would never want to hurt me again.

That's the way I deal with people who act like my horses. They might kick me or step on my toes, but I'll overlook it. Many times children treat their parents like that. They don't "get" that they're hurting the ones who are providing for them.

When Jesus was being crucified, He prayed, "Father, forgive them; for they do not know what they do."[1] What did He mean? Didn't those who crucified Him know what they were doing? In one sense, yes. But in another sense, no. If they had truly understood that He was the Son of God (and they will give an account for this horrible deed one day), they would have immediately put down their hammers and helped Him.

Jesus didn't retaliate by calling down twelve legions of angels to wipe them out. He wouldn't let them change His loving attitude or alter the mission that He was sent to Earth to accomplish. When we are being "crucified" by others' cruel remarks and actions, remember that He set an example for us to follow. Maybe if we return good for evil, love for hate, if we're nice enough to others, they will choose the right direction and serve God.

COMPARE YOUR PROBLEM WITH A MORE DESPERATE SITUATION

If you want to change your attitude, you can find a way to do it if you will try. One tactic that helps me to keep life in perspective is comparing my problems with those of someone else. When I compare my problem with someone who has an even bigger problem, I'm reminded of how good I have it. As bad as your situation may be, someone else always has it worse than you. Comparing your situation isn't to make you happy about the other person's misfortune, but to give you compassion for him and to keep your own problem in perspective. You can also compare your difficulty with a past hardship that you've experienced in your own life.

> MAYBE IF WE'RE NICE ENOUGH TO OTHERS, THEY WILL CHOOSE THE RIGHT DIRECTION AND SERVE GOD.

Several years after I retired from boxing the first time, I lost everything through some bad investments. When I was near bankruptcy, I talked to my accountants, who told me things looked grim. I knew that I needed to find a way to keep my attitude in check.

I felt compelled to drive back to my old neighborhood in Houston. We had moved frequently when I was growing up, so I drove to every house where I had lived. I sat there in my nice suit, looking at each house and reminiscing about the poverty in which I was raised.

I recalled moving into one house where the previous renters hadn't switched off their electricity. When we flipped on the light switch, we were shocked that the light came on. I was so excited that we had a light on in our house, because much of the time, our family lived without electricity. In my amazement, I kept switching the lightbulb on and off until it blew out. We were in such poverty that we didn't even own another bulb to replace it. By the time we borrowed a good light bulb, the electricity had been cut off, and we still didn't have any light. Now *that's* poor!

> COMPARE YOUR PROBLEM WITH A BIGGER PROBLEM, AND YOU'LL SEE HOW GOOD YOU HAVE IT.

We were so poverty-stricken that my mother had to decide which we needed more—gas or electricity. She couldn't afford to have both at the same time. In the winter, she paid for gas, so then we didn't have electricity. In the summer, she switched on the electricity, so then we couldn't afford gas. Sometimes we wouldn't have gas or electricity. With that in mind, imagine being depressed because you don't have a million dollars anymore!

Even though I had lost all my investments, I hadn't fallen to that stage of poverty yet. I still owned my house in Humble, Texas. I still had electricity and gas, and plenty of lightbulbs. Suddenly, my spirit got a huge boost. I put things back into perspective by comparing my current crisis with a more desperate situation. Remembering that my mother couldn't even afford a lightbulb made me realize my current situation wasn't so bad after all. I would overcome this crisis, just as I had survived growing up.

You can do the same. Take a moment to consider a bigger problem. Compare your dilemma with a worse situation, and you'll get a wake-up call about how good you really have it. Attitude is determined by how you measure things, and it will always get better if you'll magnify your blessings.

PULL OTHERS UP

Once you see how optimism lifts your spirit, you'll want others to see their situations in a positive light, too. I know many people who think the world is a bad place. They see themselves as victims and blame everyone else for causing their problems. It's hard to help those who won't change their minds.

But many others have fallen on hard times and need someone to point the way out. Some have fallen into a pit of depression. They're discouraged and desperately need someone to encourage them. They can't see all the blessings they have, but you can. Point out the good things they are blind to. Use your strength to help those who are weaker.

If a man is in a hole, I have to be *above* the situation to pull him out. I don't have to jump into the pit with him, but I can throw him a rope. I can yell, "Hey! Look up here!" When he looks up, he can have hope of getting out. People need to know that if they'll "look up" to God, He can change the way they view life.

When my mother passed away, I went to the cemetery by myself, where I broke down and cried. My wife, who was sitting in the car nearly a half mile away, called out to me, "George, are you okay?"

I wanted to say, "Listen to me cry. Can't you see that I'm hurting?" But I knew my wife and children were about to fall in the hole of grief, along with my brothers and sisters. Who was going to pull them out?

PUSH YOUR THOUGHTS AROUND INSTEAD OF LETTING THEM PUSH YOU AROUND.

I made a decision right then that I would put my crying and grief behind me. By the time my wife walked over to me, she didn't have any idea how grief-stricken I had been. It was a challenge to stay strong when I felt like falling apart, wanting everyone to commiserate with me and to pat me on the back and tell me, "It's going to be all right, George." But I knew that if I fell into the hole of grief, I'd probably pull in the rest of my family along with me. Who would pull us out? It wouldn't be the funeral director. I wanted to be the one to throw the rope to my family.

Rather than let the funeral be a depressing grief session, I decided to turn the mood around and make it a celebration of my mother's life. By an act of my will, I changed my frame of mind to focus on the plus side. Funerals have a minus and a plus side for those of us who are believers. The minus side is our loved one is no longer with us. The plus side? The person who has gone to be with the Lord is home at last in God's presence, and we'll have a grand reunion when we see each other again one day. I preached a message at my mother's funeral so everyone could see the positive side of my mother's death instead of the negative.

"Let's tell some good stories about Mother," I said. "Let's laugh together and remember the happy times with her. Mom's in heaven, and she would want us to celebrate!"

When I had my near-death experience in 1977, my greatest regret was that I hadn't said good-bye to my mother. After God gave my life back to me, I spent many years showing my love and appreciation to the woman who brought me into this world and who nurtured me and encouraged me no matter what. When I became a pastor, my mother joined my church and grew closer to the Lord. She didn't just see me as a son but also saw me as her pastor. She said, "You're my pastor now. You've been such a good son to me." When her time came, she went to be with the Lord.

God had granted me the desire of my heart—to have more time to appreciate my mother and say good-bye to her. I thought, *Now, how should I respond to that? Should I fall in the hole or celebrate her life?* I conducted the funeral with joy, and the warm feeling spread to everyone. Although we would miss her, knowing she was with the Lord set the mood to rejoice over her life.

CONTROL YOUR THOUGHTS

I heard a story about a little girl who whined and complained about everything one day. The next day, she was cheerful and sweet to everyone.

Her mother said, "Yesterday, you had such a bad attitude. Today, you're so happy. What happened?"

The little girl replied, "Yesterday my thoughts pushed me around. Today I pushed them around!"

I like that attitude! That's the key to being optimistic—push your thoughts around instead of letting them push you around. Make up your mind to think about what's good. Take control of your thoughts and decide that no matter what happens, you're going to be joyful. It's your decision. If you want to be happy, you can be happy.

A man wanted to have his picture taken with me. As I was posing, the person holding the camera said, "Come on, George. Put a *real* smile on your face."

The photographer thought I was just faking my big smile for the photo.

My son overheard his comment and replied, "Put a smile on his face? He doesn't know how to put a frown on his face!"

If you have joy in your heart, it will show up on your face. You can get a "face lift" too, if you'll just dwell on the thoughts that make you happy.

That's something to think about.

TIPS FROM GEORGE'S CORNER
ON BEING AN OPTIMIST

- Accentuate the positive and eliminate the negative.
- Look for something in every situation that brings you a little bit of happiness.
- Compare your problem with a more desperate situation.
- Help pull others out of their pits.
- Push your thoughts around instead of letting them push you around.

7
APPRECIATE TODAY

BLOOM WHERE YOU ARE PLANTED. PLAY THE HAND YOU ARE DEALT. It doesn't get any better than this! Today is as good as it gets. All of these statements are basically saying the same thing: *Appreciate today.* That is one of the most important keys to my personal success and happiness; I enjoy each day as it comes. I realize that I can't get these days back once they pass, so I no longer dream about being in another time or at a different place. Satisfaction, contentment, peace, and joy are not what I'm *going* to get but what I have right now. The key is learning to appreciate it.

Although we all know that the only moment we can actually live in is the present, our minds may tend to drift into another time period. You might be continually remembering something that happened to you ten years ago. Or you're constantly fretting about what *might* happen to you five years from now. Being preoccupied with the past or future can cause us to miss the exciting adventure of enjoying today.

When I was boxing, I traveled to numerous foreign countries. Most people would love to have toured all the places I've been. But because I was so engrossed with getting a knockout in the ring, I missed most of the fascinating sites and scenery in those nations I visited.

Jamaica, for example, has some of the most beautiful landscape, water, and beaches in the world. Strange as it may seem, when I went there, I didn't even know that the water was blue. I never saw it. The Caribbean water surrounding Jamaica is so gorgeous, warm, and inviting, and I didn't even dip my foot in it! My mind was in another world, so I missed the world in which I was living.

ENJOY EACH DAY AS IT COMES. YOU CAN'T GET THOSE DAYS BACK ONCE THEY PASS.

Then, after the boxing match was over, I simply boarded a plane and flew back to the United States. I didn't take time to tour the island, to meet some of the beautiful and gracious people who make Jamaica so special. I barely looked around while I was there, much less slowed down long enough to enjoy the place where I was working. Years later, I was talking with a friend and casually mentioned to him that I had boxed in Jamaica.

"Oh, I love the beaches of Jamaica," he said. "They have the most beautiful water there."

"They do?" I asked.

He looked at me in disbelief, wondering if I was joking.

I kicked myself for not having seen it. I was there and missed it. *Why didn't I enjoy Jamaica while I was there?* Because I hadn't yet learned the secret of enjoying every day for itself.

Similarly, I've eaten in some of the most fabulous restaurants in the world, with gourmet chefs preparing exquisite meals. Yet so often when I would dine in a fine restaurant, I missed the enjoyment of the meal or the pleasant company of my companions because I would be brooding about the fight coming up next week. The delicious food would pass right over my taste buds without me consciously tasting it. Have you ever finished a meal and could barely remember what you had just eaten? Your mind was somewhere else. That's the way I ate my meals for years.

My way of thinking completely changed after I met God. He showed me that if I wanted to enjoy my time on Earth, I needed to live differently than before. I decided I wasn't going to make the same mistakes I made my first time around. Now I was going to make the most out of each day as it came.

While making my comeback in boxing, I had an opportunity to fight in Las Vegas. I had fought there before, when I wasn't living in the light, and I had been too obsessed with boxing to enjoy anything other than the Vegas strip. During all my years of boxing, I had never gone sightseeing in any of the places where I was scheduled to fight. I learned my lesson. This time, I decided that I would get out of town and explore the incredible scenery in the area.

As I drove to see Hoover Dam, I noticed the bighorn sheep in the hills. I stopped long enough to enjoy watching those bighorn rams on the mountainside. It was a world I had never before seen. When I finally arrived at Hoover Dam, I stood amazed at that massive structure that took twenty-one thousand men and five years to build. I relished each moment of the day. Such simple pleasures, but I had always overlooked them.

That trip was a turning point for me. I decided that I was going to enjoy each moment of every day. I wasn't going to get so psyched up for a boxing match, or anything else for that matter, that I missed out on life. From then on, I was determined to live one day at a time because I'd learned my lesson: Today is as good as it gets. It doesn't get any better than right now, so I want to appreciate today.

LIVING IN THE PAST

Yesterday doesn't exist anymore, except in my memory. It's great to reminisce about *good* memories of my past. But the main reason it's a good memory is because it was enjoyable when it was "today." So learning to enjoy today has two benefits: it gives me happiness right now, and it becomes a good memory later.

Although it's fun to recall good memories, I never forget that the past is what it is—gone forever! I refuse to get trapped back there. Nostalgia is thinking that yesterday was better than today. But if I spend too much time reminiscing about "the good old days," I'll miss the fun of today. I don't want to sit around and think about how good life used to be. I like thinking about how good life is right now.

Many people have bad memories of their past that they allow to poison their present and future relationships. I've sat with lots of people and listened to their stories, and I've noticed a common thread: most of them hate something or someone in their past. They're angry about what happened or regret missing an opportunity. Some are still mad at a person who has been dead for decades. Living in the past prevents them from enjoying the present.

If there's one exercise that I've learned to practice, it's the art of letting go. I have decided that the only time I can enjoy life is right now. My children will be grown before I know it, so I need to enjoy them each day, now, while I can. Today is the only day I have when I can smell the flowers and hear the birds sing. The only time I can make the right decision or do something good for someone else is in the present.

One time I took my family to our house in the countryside. I woke my daughters up early and said, "It's time for us to watch the sunrise."

They said, "Aw, Dad. Why? It's just another day."

But I wouldn't take no for an answer. They stumbled out of bed, and we went outside to watch the sunrise. I wanted to teach them an important lesson about how to live, and I hoped they would remember it for the rest of their lives. As the sun peeked over the horizon, I told them, "This is a brand-new sunrise. You've never seen this before. I want you to understand that every day is fresh and new. It is filled with opportunities. You are not stuck in yesterday. Enjoy today and make the most of it."

> ENJOYING TODAY HAS TWO BENEFITS: IT GIVES YOU HAPPINESS RIGHT NOW, AND IT BECOMES A GOOD MEMORY LATER.

They all yawned and went back to bed, but today they still remember my point.

God is merciful and will always give us a new beginning if we are truly willing to change. I want to learn from my mistakes and not repeat them. But once I've learned what the good Lord wants me to know from those past experiences, I put them behind me. Every new day brings a new start, and that's where I want to center my attention. I don't want to miss the new sunrise.

FAST-FORWARDING TO THE FUTURE

Some people avoid living in the past, but they get tripped up by trying to live in the future, possibly dwelling on a fantasy they have concocted or a dream they hold on to but are not doing anything to bring about. He or she is thinking forward instead of backward, always living in "someday" rather than today. While we all need to plan for the future, no one needs to live there. Today is the only day we really have. Younger people are often too anxious to get into their future. They yearn for the day

> GOD IS MERCIFUL AND WILL ALWAYS GIVE US A NEW BEGINNING.

they'll drive a car, graduate school, or get married. They can't wait to reach their career goals, and in the meantime, they miss the valuable opportunities and experiences that are available only today.

Maybe your mind is stuck in fast-forward. You dislike your job, and every day you look forward to your vacation when you can finally relax. But then when the big day arrives, you can't enjoy it. The whole time you're on vacation, you're thinking about all the work you'll have to do when you get back! Your mind is stuck in fast-forward.

While anxiousness can't wait for the future and wants time to hurry up, worry expects the worst to happen and dreads the future. Both attitudes will keep you from enjoying life now. Today is as good as it gets, not tomorrow. Count the blessings that you have right now. Life is meant to be lived in the present.

To me, worrying about the future is actually a trust issue. If I'm not trusting God with my tomorrow, I'll worry about it. The twenty-third psalm says the Lord is my shepherd who will lead and take care of me. If the Lord is my shepherd, I don't need to worry about my future and how things will turn out.

The psalm goes on to say, "Surely goodness and mercy shall follow me all the days of my life."[1] God promises that goodness and mercy will *follow me* for my whole life. When I was growing up, it was the police who would always follow me! But now goodness and mercy are following me; that means everything will turn out fine, and I don't need to worry.

Instead of worrying, I release my concerns to the Lord in prayer. God invites me to cast all of my worries on Him because He cares about what I'm going through. How do I transfer my problems to God? The same way I throw a ball to someone; I have to let go of it. I release my worry by tossing it into God's hands.

Tomorrow will get here soon enough, and when it arrives, I'll call it "today." If I'm impatiently looking forward to tomorrow, I'll forfeit today's happiness.

If I'm planning a vacation, I try to enjoy every moment of the trip—the preparations, the travel, and the time I spend there when the opportunity comes, but I don't let my mind get stuck in fast-forward. When the day comes to retire, I'll enjoy that day—although I'm not planning on ever really retiring—but I don't plan to quit working until then. I try to live one day at a time, enjoying each moment, knowing I can never get that moment back. That's why I'm going to enjoy it now.

DAILY BREAD, NOT YEARLY BREAD

Have you ever wondered why Jesus taught us to pray, "Give us this day our daily bread"?[2] It's called *daily* bread because God wants us to live one day at a time. He didn't tell us to pray for yearly bread.

The Israelites wandered in the wilderness for forty years. They survived because every morning God sent them bread called manna. Every day the flaky bread would miraculously appear, looking a lot like frost on the ground. God told His people to gather up only enough for one day. If they tried to gather more, it would spoil and become uneatable.

> IT'S CALLED DAILY BREAD BECAUSE GOD WANTS US TO LIVE ONE DAY AT A TIME.

To me, the lesson is that God wants me to trust Him on a daily basis. The bread represents His provision for everything we need to live today. When we try to live more than one day at a time, life becomes hard because we're hauling around the worries and burdens of the past or the future while trying to cope with the present.

In twenty-four hours, today will become yesterday, and I can't do anything about it. Tomorrow doesn't even exist, so it does no good to worry about it. But I can do something about today, right now. I've decided that I'm going to enjoy it! I'll use it for God's honor; I'm going to live it up! I can *learn* from yesterday, and I can *look* to tomorrow. But I can only *live* in today.

That's how I get the most out of life, by cherishing each moment God has given me today.

TIPS FROM GEORGE'S CORNER
ON LIVING TODAY

- Don't be preoccupied with either the past or the future.
- Ask God to forgive your sins and trust that He did it.
- Appreciate and enjoy every moment.
- Rejoice and be glad in today.

8
GOD WILL DIRECT
YOUR STEPS

IMAGINE TRYING TO FIND BOB'S HOUSE IN NEW YORK CITY, BUT you don't have a map or a street address. You'd be pretty frustrated if you had to go knocking on every door in the city, asking if Bob lived there. It would be much easier if you had an address and a map so you could find out how to get to his house.

Many people wander aimlessly through life, unaware that God has already mapped out the best route for them. Since they don't have a purpose, they don't know why they're here on Earth. Without a destination in mind, they don't know where they're going. Consequently, they view life as a joyride, where their only aim is to have fun until they get into a wreck or have a breakdown. But the joyride never turns out to be as enjoyable as they thought.

I believe God has a plan for everyone, including you and me. He has placed you on Earth for a reason, but you won't discover it until you look to

Him. I now realize that He always had a plan for my life, even before I knew He existed. I spent my earlier years avoiding God. I wasn't ready to embrace what He wanted to do with my life. I wanted to be the boxing champion of the world and make tons of money. So He let me keep cruising on my joyride until I finally crashed at age twenty-eight.

> ## LIKE A HORSE THAT'S BEEN BROKEN, THE GOOD LORD COULD GUIDE ME WHEREVER HE WANTED ME TO GO.

When I hit the top of the boxing world, I hit the bottom at the same time. I had everything, yet I had nothing. Life was meaningless to me. I was totally empty. In desperation, I called out, "God, if You're real, maybe You can use me as something more than a boxer." It was the prayer that He had been waiting to hear.

It was as if God said, "George, are you ready to see My plan now?" Jesus came into my life in that Puerto Rican dressing room, and my life has never been the same. God's plan to use me as "more than a boxer" exceeded my wildest dreams.

Since that time, I've been a husband, father, pastor, evangelist, heavyweight champion a second time, actor, author, television commentator, commercial personality, corporate spokesman, and businessman. And I'm just getting started!

God also wants to use you in ways you can't imagine. Although you might not be called to do all the things I'm doing, rest assured that God has a wonderful plan for you that will bring peace and fulfillment. However, you can't go your way and His way at the same time. To discover His plan, you must surrender your life to Him and let Him take control of the steering wheel.

BE WILLING TO FOLLOW

At first, I didn't want anything to do with God's plan for my life. Before I knew God, I thought I knew best how to run my life, so I did whatever I pleased. I was like a wild horse being broken—bucking and kicking, trying to throw off the rider and screaming, "I want to do it *my* way."

So God let me do it my way as He patiently waited for me to come to the point of desperation. He waited for me to say, "Lord, I can't do it anymore.

I've ruined my life because I've been living recklessly. Would You please take the reins?" I had to get to the point where I was fed up with the way I had been living.

I had to come to the place where I quit kicking against God, and I ultimately surrendered to whatever He wanted to do with me. And then, just like a horse that's been broken, the good Lord could guide me wherever He wanted me to go because I finally gave up my will.

That's the place called "brokenness." When I arrived at the point of surrender, I was ready for the Master Trainer to work with me and to help me get to my new destination. I was like that wild stallion that had been firmly, but lovingly, broken by an expert trainer. I would now willingly respond to the Master's voice, following His lead.

After my conversion, I could have continued boxing. It would have been easy to do that, because fighting in the ring was all I knew. Doing anything different made me feel like a fish out of water. I was good at boxing, and that was the logical place where I seemed to fit.

I received a lot of calls from people who wanted to set up big-dollar fights for me. A few months after my loss to Jimmy Young, Ken Norton had beaten Young, so Gil Clancy called me about fighting Norton. I turned him down.

"Gil, I'm not going to box again."

"What?" he said in disbelief. "And what if I tell that to the media?"

"You can tell that to the media. I'm done with boxing."

I called Ralph Cooper, a sports writer and radio host in Houston. I told him what had happened to me in the dressing room. "I want to make an announcement on your radio show. I'm not going to box again. I'm retired." I made my retirement public so promoters would stop calling me.

Boxing wasn't what God wanted me to do at that time. I didn't understand why, but somehow, deep down inside, I knew that I had to be willing to surrender my plan to receive His plan. When I gave my life to the Lord, He totally removed all my desire to fight. I couldn't even make a fist to hit a punching bag.

After I quit boxing, I didn't have any idea what I would do next. What does a boxer do after life in the ring? All I knew was that I was willing to follow God's plan, wherever it might lead. To my surprise, ten years later,

God would lead me back into boxing, and I would once again become the world champion! More about that later, but for now, my biggest challenge was taking the next step of obedience that the Lord required of me, and that meant walking away from boxing.

THE BIGGEST FIRE IN YOUR HEART

Life is a journey to a place we've never been before. We won't always see God's finger pointing us in the direction we need to go. We may not see a road sign that says, "Congratulations. You're on the right road!" Since we don't know what the future holds, how can we move forward with certainty that we're going the right way? And how will we know that God is leading us according to His plan? All we can do is obey His Word and His voice speaking to our heart, mind, and conscience.

From the moment I first placed my trust in God, He has guided me by putting His desires in my heart. Because I'm surrendered to God's will, He puts the "fire in my heart" to want what He wants. I always know the right direction because I follow the biggest flame inside my heart. Sure, I also have a lot of little fires burning inside me, but I've learned to follow the largest flame. That is God's passion inside me, drawing me to discover what He desires.

A little flicker in my heart said, "Go after the money in boxing." Other flickers said, "What about your fame?" "What about your travel?" "What about your TV career?" Those were all little fires. But the biggest flame burning in my heart was to serve God. How? I didn't know yet. Ironically, the largest fire was the most uncertain one of all!

A verse in the hymn "His Eye Is on the Sparrow" says, "Though by the path He leads, *but one step I may see*."[1] I had only enough light to take one step. Since I didn't know where I was going, I had to take the first step by faith. That one little step was also the biggest one that I had ever taken in my life. It was in a new direction, but it was the biggest flame in my heart, and so I followed it. I had to walk one step at a time in the direction my heart was pulling. Whatever burns the brightest in my heart—that's the light I follow. That's the road I take.

When things are blurry, I know God won't ever lead me to do anything that contradicts the Bible, which is my road map to guide me through this life. I'll admit that I was never really interested in reading God's Word before I found Jesus. When I was a boy, my mother told me to read the Bible because it would make me a better person. I just looked at the pictures and then closed the book. "Wherefore art thou" didn't make sense to me.

In 1974, before I went to Africa to fight Muhammad Ali, a friend gave me a Bible to take along on my trip. He said, "George, keep this with you for good luck." I believed the Bible was just a shepherd's handbook, probably because the only verse I knew was "the LORD is my shepherd." But I was always looking for luck, so I carried that Bible with me. I had lucky pennies and good luck charms, so now I added the

THE BIGGEST FLAME BURNING IN MY HEART WAS TO SERVE GOD.

"lucky" Bible to my collection of superstitious items. After I lost the fight, I threw the Bible away. I never even opened it. I thought, *The Bible didn't help me win, so why do I need it?* I thought I'd get power simply from owning it; I didn't realize that I needed to read it and believe what it says.

Since then, I've come to understand that the Bible is my road map, not my good luck charm. It's like a light that shines on the correct path, and it has never led me down the wrong road. It has helped me make right decisions, particularly when I've read the books of Psalms and Proverbs, which are tremendously practical guides. When I've read the teachings of Jesus, I've learned the right way to respond to people. Sometimes I'll find examples in the Bible of people who were faced with decisions similar to the ones I've had to make.

By following God's promptings, I've been able to make wise decisions. The doors of opportunity that He wants me to go through have always opened in His timing. But I've also learned not to walk through just any door simply because it's open. Not every opportunity comes from God. But if I'm on the right track, He'll open some doors for me and shut others. If I'm in tune with God, I'll hear His voice in my mind and conscience, and deep within, I'll know which opportunity is right.

God's will for my life is usually confirmed by three factors: my heart's desire, agreement with God's Word, and an open door of opportunity. If those three are in harmony, I regard that as good confirmation that I'm going in the right direction. The Bible also encourages me to seek out wise counselors. If I'll walk with the wise, I will become wise as well.

CHOOSE THE RIGHT ADVISERS

Often God will guide me through the advice of wise individuals. Although I keep an open mind, I won't receive any counsel, from anyone, that goes contrary to God's Word. I'll carefully analyze the advice I receive, then discard it if it doesn't line up with the Bible. I'll never follow anyone's suggestion that points me down the wrong road. One of my favorite passages of Scripture is Psalm 1. The first verse in the book of Psalms says, "Blessed is the man who walks not in the counsel of the ungodly, nor stands in the path of sinners, nor sits in the seat of the scornful."[2] I have found that God blesses me when I listen to my godly counselors and ignore those who aren't.

> GOD'S WILL FOR MY LIFE IS USUALLY CONFIRMED BY THREE FACTORS: MY HEART'S DESIRE, AGREEMENT WITH GOD'S WORD, AND AN OPEN DOOR OF OPPORTUNITY.

Before I became a believer, I heeded some bad spiritual advice. In the 1960s, the cover of *Time* magazine asked the question, "Is God Dead?" I hadn't read the Bible, but I did read that magazine article; worse yet, I believed it.

I concluded, *Hmmm. So that's what happened to God. He died!*

My acceptance of that conclusion convinced me that God could no longer answer prayers. After all, He was dead! No wonder when I prayed for my nephew in December 1976, I said, "If there is a God, and if You are really up there like they say, and if You can help people . . ." That was the only time I tried to contact Him in all those years. After all, why would anyone ever want to pray to a dead God?

Besides, my friends told me to stay away from religion. One of the men who traveled with me said, "George, you've got to be careful with religion. Those are some bad people in church. You can get yourself into some crazy stuff." He had previously worked for the singer known as Little Richard.

"Little Richard is crazy," he said. "He told everybody he found religion.

He dropped all of his record deals and went into religion. He lost everything. Those religious people will get you to do that."

Although my friends probably meant well, their advice pushed me further away from God. That was my bad mistake, and I shouldn't have allowed it to happen, but I did. Phonies and hypocrites will always be involved in religion, but that doesn't mean that Jesus isn't real. Besides, I didn't need religion; I needed God.

Later, I chose the wrong financial advisers to invest my money, and that's why I lost it all. I made a lot of money during my boxing career. But unfortunately, I squandered away most of it because I made unwise decisions about my money, and I surrounded myself with the wrong kind of financial counsel. Almost all young athletes trust their agents, managers, or financial advisers. Since Mom and Dad aren't around to help guide their decision-making process anymore, they assume, *My manager and promoters will take care of me.* That's the way I thought, too.

One of my financial advisers said, "Hey, George, we've got this cattle ranch in Colorado as an investment opportunity for you. Put in $800,000, and you'll be set for life." Another one said, "You can't box forever, George. This investment in Louisiana gas wells will take care of you after your career is over."

Not long after I invested my money, I found out that the cattle ranch in Colorado and the gas wells in Louisiana didn't exist. One of my managers stole money out of my bank account. It was one thing after another. I trusted all those people, and every business deal they told me to invest in went under or was a scam.

A few years later, after I had become a preacher, an accountant who had blown some of my investments came to visit me to apologize for losing my money. He brought a big guy along to protect himself, assuming I would beat him up. I had been a preacher for a number of years, but he still thought I was the old George and was afraid of me. What hurt me more than losing my money was that he didn't believe I had actually changed and was truly serving the Lord.

I forgave him for everything and put it behind me. But if I had to do it all over again, I never would have listened to his advice or let him invest my money. That's why, when I now seek advice, I make sure it's from godly, wise people.

My mother taught me many tidbits of wisdom. Numerous times she told me, "A liar *will* steal." Mom was right! If a person isn't truthful in what he says, he'll be dishonest in other areas as well. I think she learned that from personal experience. Another one of her favorite sayings was, "God may not answer the moment you call Him, but He's always right on time." She meant that God's timing is different from ours; He knows exactly what we need, when we need it, and He's never late.

When I was growing up, Mom told me it was better to walk away from a street fight than to get killed. She often cautioned, "It's better to say, 'There he goes,' than 'There he lays.'" Even though it was good advice, I had never walked away from a fight and didn't plan to in the future.

One day I heard that a friend of mine had been beaten up with brass knuckles by a neighborhood thug named Murdoch. Vicious and violent, Murdoch had been known to kill people and always carried a knife with a hook on it, similar to the tool carpet layers use to cut rugs. He worked with another guy who would sneak up behind the target and crack him over the head with a board before Murdoch cut him open.

I decided to find Murdoch and repay him for beating up my friend. I asked around, but never could find him. One night, I was at a party and decided to walk outside to get some fresh air. As I sat on the porch alone, Murdoch and his cohort sauntered out of the shadows, where they had been lurking. Everybody inside the house was dancing and not paying attention to what was happening outside on the porch.

Murdoch pulled out his knife and said, "Man, I heard you were looking for me." His accomplice nervously waved his stick, getting ready to hit me. I couldn't tend to both of them at the same time.

Again he said, "Were you looking for me?"

Just when I was getting ready to hit him, I heard my mother's voice in my mind. "*It's better to say, 'There he goes' than 'There he lays.'*" I immediately knew that I needed to back down.

As he gritted his teeth, he asked me again, "Are you looking for me, man?"

"No," I answered. "I'm not looking for you." I felt like a coward for backing down, but if I hadn't, I probably would have been killed. I credit my mother's wise saying for saving my life that night.

Murdoch and his sidekick turned around and left. Murdoch had never before let anyone off the hook. I now realize that God spared my life through my listening to wise counsel.

Sometimes God directs us through circumstances involving other people. That's what happened to me about six years after I'd retired from boxing. I was quite content with my new life, serving God along with a small congregation in Houston, and I never wanted to have anything further to do with boxing. I had found peace working with the church, and I was happy preaching and telling others about the good Lord.

Then one day I was visiting my brother Roy, who was working with kids in a boxing gym in Houston. During the heyday of my boxing career, Roy had worked with me, taking care of my business concerns. In return, I gave him a percentage of my boxing purses, which at times was a considerable amount of money. But like me, Roy had not wisely invested his earnings, and by the early 1980s, he was flat broke. He was back home, living with our mother, working odd jobs, and volunteering his time teaching kids how to box at a decrepit gymnasium owned by a local

WHEN I SEEK ADVICE, I MAKE SURE IT'S FROM GODLY, WISE PEOPLE.

church. Ironically, Roy had never been a boxer, but he had worked closely with me over the years, listening to my trainers and studying other boxers as well as me. And he had learned enough about boxing to be a good teacher, especially for the young beginners. No doubt, they respected his advice as the brother of the former heavyweight champion of the world.

When I stopped by to encourage Roy, he was preparing to work with some of the young boys in the ring. Several mothers were registering their boys for the program, so I waved a quick hello. I overheard one of the parents say, "Oh, look, that's George Foreman. If you sign up your son, George can help him." When they saw me, one of the moms gave me a look as if to say, "George Foreman could really help my son stay out of trouble."

But I was having none of that. I knew my congregation would be upset if they thought I was involved in boxing again, so I returned the woman's look with an expression that said, "I'm a preacher, and if you want help for your son, send him to church." I left the gym, thinking that I'd never return.

Some time later, I was with Roy again when that boy and his mother came to mind. "What ever happened to that boy?" I asked Roy after describing the look his mom had given me.

"Oh, George, that kid went to prison," Roy said, shaking his head.

"What? Prison?" I was truly shocked. I could still see the boy standing near me in the gym. "You've got to be kidding."

"No, he robbed a convenience store along with one of his friends," Roy said sadly. "The storekeeper shot the boy's friend, so the kid from the gym shot the storekeeper."

"And killed him?" I was almost too afraid to ask.

"No, but he hurt him real bad, though."

I was devastated by the news. Making matters worse, I discovered that the store the young boxer had robbed was located in Humble, Texas, right down the road from my home.

I couldn't help beating myself up over the missed opportunity. I may have had a chance at turning that young man's life around, but I had been so worried about what my good church members would think of me for helping a boy learn to box, I had ignored the need right in front of me. Now all those lives were devastated—at least partly because I was more worried about my reputation than I was about helping that young man. I was extremely upset and ashamed of myself.

I told Roy, "We've got to do something to help these kids. If we just had a place where they could come. . . ." I thought of a large warehouse down the street from my church. The building had been abandoned by the contractor before it was completed. It would take a sizable amount of money to purchase, renovate, and furnish the building, but by now, thanks to my unwise investments and a series of unwise relationships, I was struggling to make ends meet financially myself, let alone able to contribute a large sum of money to help a bunch of kids I didn't even know.

I decided there was only one thing to do. I had a retirement fund, my life's savings, part of which I had already tapped into, so I took that money and, with Roy's help, formed a charitable foundation that bought the warehouse, refurbished it, and furnished it with weights, boxing gloves, a basketball court, and the boxing ring that we pulled out of my ranch in Marshall. We named the place the George Foreman Youth and Community Center.

From the day we opened the doors, the kids started coming. Because of my belief that kids need to understand that everything costs something, that there really are no free lunches in life, we charged the kids one dollar for every year of their age—a ten-year-old paid $10 per year; a thirteen-year-old paid $13 per year. Roy and I worked with the kids, but most of all, we just loved them and accepted them. I didn't want our youth center to be overladen with rules and regulations; our main rules were to play fair and demonstrate good sportsmanship.

I remembered some of the community efforts in my own neighborhood to reach kids that I had rejected as a boy. Many of those efforts were the results of sincerely concerned Christians and other civic-minded people who truly wanted to help. But they were so heavy-handed with their message that they drove kids away before the adults ever earned the right to be heard and to build good relationships. I avoided those places, as did most of my friends.

I wanted the George Foreman Youth and Community Center to be different. I decided that I would never preach to the kids; I would show them my faith by my works. They would see God in my life as a result of how I acted and how I responded to other people's actions, not just by what I said. My role was simply to be there for the boys, to be available to talk with them, to watch them as they played basketball or lifted weights or boxed. I walked around the center and tried to encourage the boys every way I could. "Nice shot!" "That's the way to work on that punching bag." "You're doing a good job."

Funding the youth center was a formidable problem. Just making the mortgage payment was difficult enough, not to mention maintaining the place, paying for the utilities, and providing the equipment we needed. I kept siphoning money off my savings until there was little left. I kept hoping that something would happen to solve our financial problems, but nothing did.

Sometimes reality pokes a hole in the balloon of our idealism. That happened to me when my attorney who had set up my financial affairs visited the center and sounded a warning. "George, I know you want to help these kids, but you can't afford to keep up the youth center. If you don't make some changes soon, you're going to end up like Joe Louis, broke and out on the streets shaking hands with people, trying to make a dollar. You are going to have to pull back."

I refused to give up on the youth center. I accepted several speaking invitations and used the honorariums to help pay for the center's expenses. Those speaking engagements and my dwindling life's savings were all that I had to keep the doors to the youth center open. I didn't want to ask the government for money, and I certainly didn't want to go around begging the public for donations.

I spoke at a Christian conference in Georgia, after which the conference organizer got up and made an impassioned plea for money to help the George Foreman Youth and Community Center. I sat on the speakers' platform throughout the pitch, and the longer the fellow went on, the more embarrassed I became. I hadn't come to the conference to beg for money or to try to milk donations out of the participants who had already paid dearly to attend the event. I decided then and there that I would find another way to raise the necessary funds. Then it hit me: *I know how I can get the money we need. I'm going to fight for it. I'm going to be the heavyweight champion of the world—again—and this time, I will do things right.*

> I CAN'T TRULY ENJOY OBEYING GOD UNLESS I'M REALLY IN LOVE WITH HIM.

On another occasion, I went to New York City to receive an award and ran into Art Linkletter. I had been experiencing some difficulties and needed some good advice. Art looked me in the eye and said, "George, I've heard about how you're helping all those kids at the George Foreman Youth Center in Houston. Just keep doing good and good will come to you."

I needed to hear those words: *Keep doing good, and good will come to you.* The good thing is usually the right thing. It's not hard to figure out. If I'll do good, then blessings will come back to me. God will make sure of it. Whatever I sow, I'll reap. If I sow a good seed, I'll reap a good harvest. So I've learned that if I make the right decisions every day, I'll always be pleased with the results later.

TRUST AND OBEY

I constantly try to give my children good advice, but they don't always understand it. That's when they need to trust me. They have to put their faith in me and believe that as their father, I want only the best for them. They obey me—even when they don't understand—because they love me.

The same concept applies to my relationship with God. He loves me and always wants the best for me. But I must trust Him, even when I don't fully understand. If I always knew the outcome of every one of my situations, I'd never need to trust God. Trust means I believe in the character of the good Lord and I'm confident that He will do what's right, even when my circumstances don't make sense to me.

Sometimes God gives instructions that go against conventional wisdom, such as treating people kindly when they're hateful. Who really wants to do that? Instructions like that may not always make sense, so that's why I need to trust and obey the One who inspired them. Obedience is simply trusting God. King Solomon said, "Trust in the LORD with all your heart, and lean not on your own understanding; in all your ways acknowledge Him, and He shall direct your paths."[3]

I can't truly enjoy obeying God unless I'm really in love with Him. If ever I'm obedient merely out of a sense of duty or obligation, without being in love, it becomes a dreaded drudgery. But when I obey from my heart and put my whole heart in it, I'm obeying Love. And that's the way God wants me to serve Him—as an act of love.

PRAY FOR GUIDANCE

When someone asks me, "Where do you get good advice?" I tell them, "Down on my knees!" Prayer is simply talking with God and allowing Him the opportunity to communicate with me. If I don't know what to do in a situation, I just remember that the Lord has all the answers I need. He hears my prayers and will send His messages as thoughts in my mind and impressions in my heart. Often He'll remind me of something that I've read in His Word. Sometimes He may use a song, a sermon, or something in nature—a flower, a mountain, or a river—to speak to my heart, mind, and conscience.

I try to find a private place to get alone each day and talk with God for an hour. The length of time I pray isn't nearly as important as the attitude of my heart. I always make sure that I'm being sincere when I pray and not just saying words out of ritual. If I'm praying for wisdom, sometimes the answers I need will pop into my mind. That's one way God speaks to me.

One day my wife, Mary, was praying alone when the Lord spoke to her: "Ask Me what you want."

She said, "Lord, I want George to be heavyweight champion of the world again, and please restore his car collection and everything else that his investers lost."

God spoke to her heart, "He'll have it."

That was the confirmation I needed. The Lord led me back to boxing again in 1987, which was ten years after I had retired. Why would God lead me back into boxing? Because through that avenue He would not only provide my financial needs, but also open many new doors to help people. This time I learned how to box as a sport, without hating my opponents, which was different from the way I had fought before I'd trusted the Lord with my life.

As I resumed my boxing career, I continued to be pastor of my church in Houston. Have you ever heard of a boxing preacher? Well, that was me. The Lord certainly moves in mysterious ways!

I had just started my comeback, and we were barely getting by financially because of my previous bad investments. Mary told me, "As I was praying, the Lord told me you would be champion of the world again and He would restore everything you once had."

When she said that, two things impressed me. First, it humbled me that her prayer was for me and not herself. She felt that I had lost all the things I once owned. Second, she firmly believed that God had made her a promise, and nothing would convince her otherwise. I needed to hear that word from God, so I kept that promise in my mind to keep from getting discouraged.

In 1991 it appeared that my time had come. After four years of boxing, I was scheduled to fight Evander Holyfield for the heavyweight championship of the world. I was certain that I would win the boxing match and become the new champion, fulfilling the promise that God had given Mary. I was now forty-two years old, and it looked like this would be my only opportunity to regain the title.

I boxed all twelve rounds against a rock-solid man thirteen years younger than me, but lost the fight on the judges' scorecards. I just couldn't understand it. Why did I lose? Had God really spoken to my wife, or did she just *think* she heard from God? I appreciated her faith in God and her confidence in me, but I was the guy getting pounded in the boxing ring!

Even after the loss, Mary's faith wasn't shaken. She said, "George, all I know is what God told me. You're going to be the heavyweight champion again."

"Okay, Mary. I'll keep training."

In 1993 I had another opportunity to fight for the heavyweight title against Tommy Morrison. I was convinced this *had* to be the fulfillment of the promise. I was now forty-four years old fighting a twenty-five-year-old. Again I lost on the judges' scorecards. I was disappointed, but I had just signed a contract to do a television sitcom, so I didn't sit around wallowing in despair. I kept busy.

Mary, however, still didn't back down. "George, you're going to be champion again."

In 1994 I was offered one more shot at the title against Michael Moorer. I was now forty-five years old; no professional fighter had ever won the World Boxing Association heavyweight title at my age. But this time would be different. I'll fill you in on the details in a later chapter, but for now, I'll just say I won the fight and recaptured the title as the world's heavyweight champion. God had spoken to Mary after all!

SOMETIMES THE ANSWERS I NEED WILL POP INTO MY MIND.

After I won, she came up to me with a big grin on her face and said, "I *told you* what God said, didn't I?" Incidentally, the Lord restored my car collection—one of my favorite hobbies—as well, as a reminder that when God restores, He gives back double what was lost! And along the way, we earned enough money to pay off the mortgage on the George Foreman Youth and Community Center and to set up an endowment fund to finance the upkeep and refurnishing of the center for a long time to come.

God may be asking you to do some things that seem impossible, just like He asked of me. You can do it, too, if you'll hold on to His promises and continue to be faithful. And when it comes to pass, don't forget to give Him the credit.

KEEP BEING FAITHFUL

When I made my comeback in boxing, my church was still my higher priority. I would not neglect my responsibilities as pastor, even with my busy schedule. After each fight, people would beg me to stay for certain post-fight events. I'd tell them, "I'm sorry, but I can't hang around. I've got to hurry to get back to my church!"

I didn't get much sleep on those nights that I fought. After boxing on Saturday night, I would catch a late flight back to Houston, getting back just in time to make it to church so I could preach. I wanted my congregation to know that although I had fought in front of millions of people on television the night before, they were my most important audience.

AFTER BOXING ON SATURDAY NIGHT, I WOULD CATCH A LATE FLIGHT BACK TO HOUSTON SO I COULD PREACH.

Sometimes I looked rather funny as I preached wearing sunglasses to cover up my swollen eyes. After church one Sunday, some kids came up and asked, "Can we see? Can we see? Will you take off your sunglasses so we can see your eyes?"

"Are you sure you want to see them?" I asked.

"Yeahhhh!" they yelled together.

When I took off the glasses, revealing the black and blue puffy skin around my eyes, they hooted and hollered. They said, "You look like the cowardly lion in *The Wizard of Oz!*"

No matter what God leads me to do, I'll be faithful to my calling. I don't worry about what others say about me. I might look like the cowardly lion to them. But in God's eyes, I'm the heavyweight champion. And if God is in your corner, so are you.

TIPS FROM GEORGE'S CORNER
ON FOLLOWING GOD

- Surrender your will to God so He can lead you to the right places.
- Read the Bible; it is your roadmap through life.
- Follow the biggest flame burning in your heart.
- Choose wise and godly people to advise you.
- Trust the Lord and obey what He tells you to do.

9

THE WORST THING CAN BE THE BEST THING

I SOMETIMES WONDER, *WHAT WOULD HAVE HAPPENED IF I HAD WON my fights against Jimmy Young and Muhammad Ali?* I can see myself proudly raising my hands in victory, the reporters pushing their microphones in front of my face, hoping for some sound bite that might make the next broadcast or deadline. I can hear myself boasting to them, "You see? *I* am the greatest boxer of all time, not Ali!" And then I would have continued traveling down the road to destruction.

But as I look back, I can honestly tell you that I'm now happy about those losses. They weren't what I wanted or what I would have chosen if given a choice, but those losses were part of God's plan for my life. What looked like the worst thing that could have happened to me turned out to be the best thing. I needed to suffer those defeats so I could hit bottom and look up.

As I reflect on my life, I've noticed that simple truth showing up again and again: What looks like the worst disaster can turn into the greatest blessing—if you'll give God first place in your life. It's a spiritual paradox; losing can actually be winning. You won't be able to see it, though, as you go through the trial. It's not until later—sometimes much later—when you look back and connect the dots, that you can see God's hand at work.

Why would God want you to lose? It may be that He's trying to point you to something that's more important. It could be He wants you to reevaluate your life. Perhaps He's changing your direction. Maybe He has something better planned for you, but it's hidden right now, or perhaps you aren't quite ready to receive what He has for you.

If you love God, He promises to bring something good out of everything that happens to you. The Bible says, "And we know that all things work together for good to those who love God, to those who are the called according to His purpose."[1] That verse doesn't promise that only good things will happen to you. It doesn't mean that you'll always escape trouble, that you'll never lose a fight (or a job, or a mate), or that no one will ever betray you. It does mean that God is in control; He can turn any situation around and work it out for your good. Not everything that happens to you will *be* good, but God can *make* it into something good.

Understand, He will not take away anyone's free will, which is one reason why so many bad things happen in the first place. Don't blame God when people choose to do evil. Even so, the Lord sees your misfortunes before they occur and *plans ahead* to make something good come out of them. He turns your enemies' evil intentions around for His purposes and creates a great ending in your situation. Although you can't understand how He does it, give Him credit for being smarter than you! He's wiser than your enemies and more powerful than your circumstances.

> LOSING CAN ACTUALLY BE WINNING, BUT YOU WON'T BE ABLE TO SEE IT UNTIL YOU LOOK BACK AND CONNECT THE DOTS.

To me, one of the clearest biblical examples of this is demonstrated in the life of Joseph. When he was seventeen years old, his hateful brothers threw him into a pit in the wilderness. When some Ishmaelite traders passed by, Joseph's brothers pulled him out and sold him for some quick cash. The traders transported him to Egypt, where they sold him as a slave to a man named Potiphar, who was Pharaoh's officer. Even though Joseph faithfully served in the palace, Potiphar's wife falsely accused him of attacking her. Without a trial, Joseph was declared guilty and locked up in prison.

Although it looked like Joseph's circumstances were out of control, the Bible tells us that "the LORD was with him."[2] After interpreting a dream for Pharaoh, Joseph was released from prison and, amazingly, was promoted to second in command over Egypt. Through his position as a ruler, God used him to save the nation of Israel during a time of famine.

> NOT EVERYTHING THAT HAPPENS TO YOU WILL BE GOOD, BUT GOD CAN MAKE IT GOOD.

When he was reunited with his brothers many years later, he said, "You meant evil against me, but *God meant it for good* in order to bring about the present result, to preserve many people alive."[3] God used every attack on Joseph as a stepping-stone to take him to a higher position.

Just as God turned around bad things for good in Joseph's life, He can do the same for you. I've had four significant losses in my life that looked like the worst things that could have possibly happened to me, but they all turned out to be stepping-stones to greater success, influence, and contentment. Consider these four losses that God turned into victories in my life.

1. THE LOSS TO MUHAMMAD ALI

When I lost the fight to Muhammad Ali, it devastated me because I was no longer the world's champion. Imagine losing everything you think matters to you in ten seconds. I thought my life was over, so I plunged into depression. Nothing satisfied; nothing could pull me out of the downward spiral I felt taking place in my life.

But after I found Christ, I could look back on that boxing match and actually thank God. Although I didn't know it at the time, what seemed to be the worst thing was actually the best thing. Why? Because that loss started me on my search for God.

In 1978 I was working in the field on my ranch in Marshall, Texas, when a sports reporter stopped by for an interview. He was going to New Orleans to see Muhammad Ali fight for the title for the third time.

"What happened during your fight with Ali in Africa?" he asked, expecting me to make up an excuse for losing.

"I lost," I replied straightforwardly. "I've got the picture of me on the canvas that proves I got beat."

The reporter asked, "But what about the loose ropes in the ring that Ali kept leaning back on?"

Muhammad Ali had nicknamed our fight "Rope-a-Dope" because he leaned back on the loose ropes so often to avoid my punches. I kept swinging at him until I reached the point of exhaustion. Of course, I was the "dope"—in more ways than one, I later realized when I recalled the fuss over my pre-fight drink of water. (I now believed I had been drugged by the medicinal-tasting water just before the fight.)

"The best man won and I lost," I said. "But I want to tell you something. That was a fight where God was with me, and the devil was trying to get me. It was good versus evil, and God won."

I was trying to explain to him about the *spiritual battle* that I was fighting inside my soul, and that losing the fight was an important step in George Foreman finding God. But the sportswriter misunderstood what I was trying to say.

When the article was published, I was shocked to read, "George said that when he fought Ali, it was a fight of God against the devil." That wasn't what I said, nor was it my intended meaning, but that's how he wrote it.

One of Ali's trainers, who read that article, retorted, "Yes, it was God versus the devil, and God won" (meaning Ali).

He didn't realize what he was saying. God did win, because it led to my finding Jesus Christ. If I had won that boxing match against Ali, I'm not sure I ever would have found Jesus and received eternal life.

GOD WANTED ME TO LOSE THAT FIGHT, SO THAT I COULD LOSE MY LIFE.

Of course, God could have struck me dead in the dressing room after the Ali fight instead of after the Jimmy Young bout. But the timing wasn't right. I first needed to go through my time of devastation and depression. I had to see that I had nothing to live for so that I could come to the end of myself. I discovered, for the first time, that wealth didn't solve my problems. No preacher could have told me that at the time and expected me to understand. I had to find that out. God had to show me that nothing I owned could lift my depression or bring peace to my mind.

It was the first time in my professional boxing career that I had been defeated, and nothing on Earth could fill that void. I knew something was missing in my life. Before I could find the "something" that I was looking for, I had to die to my old life. I was like a grain of wheat that had to die in the ground before new life could come out of it.

All the pieces of the puzzle had to come together. I couldn't find life until I first reached a point of desperation. And that's why losing to Ali was one of the best things that ever happened to me.

2. THE LOSS TO JIMMY YOUNG

After losing to Ali, I won the next five fights in a row, all by knockouts. Winning my next fight against Jimmy Young would pave the way for another shot at Muhammad Ali. Although I was a heavy favorite to win, I lost the fight. And just like before, I thought my defeat was the worst thing that could have happened to me. But again it turned out to be the best thing.

It wasn't but a few minutes after this loss that I died in the dressing room and had my vision of Jesus Christ being crucified. God wanted me to lose that fight so that I could lose my life. That's not an excuse; that's the truth! Losing my life became the best thing that ever happened to me because that's when I found God.

If it were possible to go back in time and turn those losses to wins, I'd say, "No way!" I would never change those outcomes. If I had beaten Ali and Young, I never would have hit bottom and found Jesus as a result. I had to lose on Earth so I could win in heaven.

When I was out of my body in that dark place, it seemed like a dimension outside of time. But I was there long enough to know it was a real place—a place of utter hopelessness. Then God gave me my life back and revealed Himself to me. When I saw the vision of the blood on my hands and forehead, I had no doubt that Jesus Christ was the Son of God; He was the One I had been looking for all my life, and I hadn't even realized it prior to that experience.

I walked out of that dressing room with peace of mind for the first time in my life. I had never ever felt that wonderful! Suddenly, money wasn't important. Fame and status meant zero to me. Everyone needs to come to that place where they die to themselves and their own ways. It's only then that we find what we really need.

I ALSO MADE A BIGGER POINT—THAT GOD CAN TURN ANY LOSS INTO A GAIN.

I've told my testimony about my death experience all over the world. I've spoken about it to tens of thousands of people at one time. If just one person comes to know Jesus as a result of my glimpse of utter darkness, it will have been worth my terrifying time there.

3. THE LOSS OF MY INVESTMENTS

Before I retired from boxing, I had made millions of dollars. But just a few years later, it was all gone. A friend I depended on sold my house and all its contents without my knowledge, an accountant stole my money, and others I trusted made shady investments. I foolishly put everything I owned in their hands and then watched it all disappear.

Every time I thought about their stealing from me, I reminded myself, *They may have my money, but I've got God's grace, and that's sufficient for me.* I didn't get depressed over losing the money, because I never really "owned" it anyway. Everything I have belongs to God.

What good could come out of losing my investments? It forced me to make a comeback in boxing, which opened up far more doors for ministry and business than I ever had before. If I hadn't lost my money, I would not have returned to boxing and would have missed all the opportunities and assignments that God had planned for me.

4. THE LOSS TO EVANDER HOLYFIELD

My fourth major loss resulted from my fight with Evander Holyfield for the heavyweight title. In 1991 I was making my comeback and was scheduled to battle Holyfield for $12.5 million. Everyone said I was way too old to be fighting at age forty-two; reporters quipped that I should be in an old folks' home rather than in a boxing ring. In spite of their jokes, I was determined to win the fight. The bout went the entire twelve rounds, and I lost on points on the judges' scorecards.

At the post-fight press conference, a reporter asked me if I was upset about losing on points. I replied, "I lost by a few points, but I sure made a big point. *Age forty is not a death sentence!*"

When I made that statement, the whole world opened up to me. Almost overnight, it seemed like every advertiser on television wanted to hire me for their commercials. Interesting, isn't it? They didn't ask the winner to be in the commercials—they asked the loser! I received invitations to be on talk shows. I even starred in my own television show called *George*.

I believe the point resonated with the public—no one is ever too old to take on a new challenge. Although I didn't win the boxing match, I gained the world's respect by showing that most of the limitations on success in our society are self-imposed. The only person who could have kept me from competing for the championship that I felt God wanted me to have was me! I wasn't about to limit God, and I sure didn't want to limit me.

But I also made a more important point—that God can turn any loss into a gain. If the Lord is with you, He can take any defeat that you've suffered and make it into a situation where you'll benefit.

Although you've probably never lost a boxing match, you may have experienced a loss in other ways. Perhaps you've been fired from a job. Maybe your spouse abandoned you, leaving you with children to raise and bills to pay. Possibly you have lost money in your investments. It doesn't matter who you are, sooner or later, you'll be faced with a loss.

In the Bible, Job was an honorable man in every way, but he lost almost everything he had through a series of horrible tragedies. But in the end, God turned the worst into the best and restored and doubled everything Job lost.

Remember how Joseph was sold into slavery by his jealous brothers? In Joseph's case, God took him from the pit to the palace; He turned the worst into the best; He made the prisoner and slave into a powerful ruler. And He can turn the worst into the best in your situation, too.

Don't let questions about the outcome of your situation turn you into a nervous wreck. Keep trusting, believing, and taking the next step of obedience that the good Lord shows you. God usually doesn't want us to know too much about what's going on behind the scenes or how He plans to work things out for our good. He wants us to trust Him. If you knew all that your future held, you wouldn't need faith. Just take one step at a time, trusting that God still has a plan for you, and He will make the best out of your situation.

YOUR WORST ENEMY CAN BECOME YOUR BEST FRIEND

You already know how much I hated Muhammad Ali after losing to him. But you don't know the rest of the story. About two months after my conversion, I called Muhammad Ali to let him know what happened to me in the dressing room. During our conversation, he made me an offer.

"George, I'll give you another shot at the title, but on one condition. You will first need to fight Ken Norton and beat him."

I thanked him for the opportunity but told him I wasn't interested. "Thanks, Muhammad, but I don't want another shot at the title. I've found Jesus Christ, and I'm going to live for God and trust Him with my future."

He thought I should keep fighting since he had been boxing in the name of his religion. "Live for God?" he asked. "But what about Samson? Wasn't he the strongest man in the Bible?"

"I'm sorry, Muhammad; I'm hanging up the gloves. But I want you to know that I'll be there for you if you ever need me."

Up to this point, we had been enemies. But he responded to my kindness and called me back. As we got to know each other, a friendship developed between us. The man who had been my worst enemy was calling me on the phone nearly every day!

He'd write letters to me and jokingly sign them, "Love, Muhammad Ali." I'd reply and pay him back with, "Love, George."

Ali couldn't believe how much my attitude had changed after I found Christ. As we talked about God, he would ask, "But what about this? What about that?" He listened to my beliefs and always came up with a tricky question about the Bible. He knew that something had changed my life and finally acknowledged that I must have truly found the Lord.

In my trophy case, I have a photograph on display that was taken during our fight in Africa. The picture shows me being knocked down and Ali standing over me as the referee is getting ready to count. That photo is showcased so everyone can see the picture first, before viewing any other award. Why? It was the moment that started my search for God.

As I've gazed at the picture that captured my first professional defeat, I've fallen in love with that moment. And I've learned to love that man— the one I had hated so much. I now understand that it really wasn't just Muhammad Ali who knocked me down after all. God orchestrated my downfall to get me where I am today.

The worst thing had become the best thing. And Muhammad Ali, who had been my worst enemy, actually became one of my best friends.

It doesn't matter what your "worst" is. It could be the worst decision you've ever made. The worst enemy you've ever had. The worst disaster you've ever experienced.

What does matter is that you place your worst in the Lord's hands and let Him make the best of it.

TIPS FROM GEORGE'S CORNER ON TURNING THE WORST INTO THE BEST

- Don't be bitter about the losses you've experienced.
- Look for God's purpose in your circumstances.
- Trust the Lord that He will make something good out of your situation.

10
INSPIRING OTHERS TO EXCELLENCE

ONE OF MY GOALS IS TO INSPIRE EVERYONE I MEET TO BECOME A better person. You'd be surprised how a few words of encouragement can revolutionize the way a person thinks about himself. A man by the name of Carl Hempe gave a thirty-minute speech in 1965 that changed how I viewed myself and inspired me to excellence. Before I tell you what he said, you first need to understand a bit about Carl's background.

Carl Hempe's father, Frederick, was a high-ranking German officer who was captured by American troops during World War I. Frederick was brought to the United States and placed in a prisoner of war camp in New York. After the war, he was so impressed by America that he immigrated to the United States. He became an American citizen, got married, and started a family.

When World War II broke out, Frederick's son, Carl, joined the United States Army and served under General George Patton. Ironically, the son of the former German officer was fighting as an American against Adolf Hitler's regime. Despite his German heritage, Carl's allegiance was to the United States.

In 1965 I joined the Job Corps to receive training for a vocation. Most of the teenagers in the Corps had come off the streets and were searching to find our identity. Carl came to the center to give us some words of encouragement. He explained that his father had fought for Germany but later left his country so he could become an American citizen. Then Carl looked me right in the eye and said, "You're getting into trouble because people are calling you names. You're *an American*. That's your name, and don't ever forget it!"

I had been called a lot of things, but no one had ever called me an American before. In the 1960s, many people were protesting against our country, and for a while, it seemed that national pride was at an all-time low. But Carl's words penetrated my heart, and for the first time in my life, I felt proud to be an American.

Three years later, I represented the United States as a boxer in the 1968 Olympics. Many American athletes had boycotted the games to make a political statement, and tension filled the air. But I never forgot that speech I heard while in the Job Corps.

My heavyweight match for the gold medal was against a representative from America's most ominous enemy at that time, Russia. I defeated the Russian boxer and achieved my greatest dream in that season of life—winning an Olympic gold medal. After the fight, I did something that startled the viewers who watched on their television sets. Instead of protesting, I walked around the ring, waving a small American flag for the entire world to see. I proudly waved the flag when it wasn't popular to do so because Carl Hempe told me, "You're an American, and don't ever forget it!"

Years later, in May 2006, I spoke at a high school graduation in Nacogdoches, Texas. As I had done so many times over the last forty years, I shared how Carl Hempe's speech had changed my life. After the ceremony, a newspaper reporter interviewed me and wrote a story about Carl that was eventually posted on the Internet.[1]

Someone read the article and informed the eighty-five-year-old Carl Hempe how much his speech had impacted my life. He had *no idea* that his talk to a small group of teenagers in 1965 would be repeated again and again to thousands of people all over the world. It wasn't until forty years later that he heard about his harvest from the seed he planted in a troubled teenager.

Carl Hempe inspired me to be a better person, and I am determined to pass along the favor. But before I could help others, I first needed to learn a lesson myself.

MY LESSON AT IHOP

Even though I'm a pastor, I need to be preached to myself every now and then. I'm blind to my own faults and need someone to point them out to me. One of the best sermons I ever heard was preached at the International House of Pancakes (IHOP).

NO ONE HAD EVER CALLED ME AN AMERICAN BEFORE.

While I was training for the heavyweight title against Evander Holyfield, I stopped eating my favorite high-calorie foods to get my weight down for the match. I was always hungry during my training and looked forward to rewarding myself with a big meal after the bout.

I told my wife, "After the fight, we're going to IHOP, and I'm going to order everything I'm starving for—pancakes and syrup, bacon, eggs, sausage, orange juice . . ." I so hungered to eat this meal that I marked it on my calendar.

After the match, we went to the restaurant as we had planned. While I was devouring my meal, a fan spotted me and walked up to our table.

"George Foreman! Would you sign an autograph for me?"

I didn't want to be interrupted. I just wanted to eat my food.

"Could you wait? As soon as I get through eating, I'll do it."

"Okay," he replied and walked away disappointed.

Mary laid down her fork and stared at me in disbelief. Then she preached the message that I'll never forget.

"Look, George. Everybody thinks you're the nicest guy in the world because you're smiling in all those commercials. But you wouldn't stop eating for fifteen seconds to sign an autograph for that man. You can't treat people like that. So you either *be* the nicest guy, or don't be! But don't pretend to be one person and act like another!"

Her words hit me harder than a Holyfield punch. I hadn't realized how snobbish I must have appeared. That was one of the best sermons I had ever heard, and I repented on the spot!

Immediately I yelled to the guy, "Hey! Come back!"

The man came back to our table, and I chatted with him as I gave him my autograph. I wanted him to know he wasn't a bother, as I might have made him feel earlier. I had learned my lesson about treating everyone with dignity.

Ever since then, I've tried to make everyone feel important. When I'm going through the airport, I'm often stopped by people who want to talk with me. As I look for my gate, they'll call out, "Hey, George Foreman!" Even if I'm in a hurry, I'll stop to talk with strangers as though we were old friends. I'll ask about their family and how they're doing. I'll let them know how much I appreciate their support and prayers.

If I get delayed and miss my plane, I can always catch another flight. But I don't want to miss the opportunity to inspire someone to be a better person.

VIEW EVERYONE AS IMPORTANT

Years ago, I attended a boxing match where a popular actor was in attendance. Mike Tyson was fighting for the championship, and a number of celebrities were in the audience that evening. As the actor strutted down the aisle into the arena, people started calling out his name and tried to shake his hand. He gave them the cold shoulder and wouldn't so much as look their way. It's sad, but some celebrities will act rude to their fans because they see them as nuisances. When I saw him stick his nose up at the crowd, I thought, *Lord, please don't ever let me treat people like that.*

I've attended other sporting events where I've seen fans walk up to popular athletes and ask for their autographs. Many times the superstars will respond with a "get out of my face" attitude. They treat their adoring fans as intruders who are invading their space.

That's no way to behave toward people. Most fans are just trying to show respect. Because some athletes don't know how to interact with folks properly, I try to set an example for them to follow.

When I go into a boxing arena to work as a television commentator, I'll hear people chanting, "George! George! George!" If at all possible, I'll take some time with the spectators to sign autographs, give hugs, and have my picture taken with them.

Sometimes other athletes see me warming up to my fans, and they realize that's how they want to treat their admirers, too. Soon I'll hear them saying, "Sure, I'll sign an autograph for you." And then I smile because my behavior has rubbed off on them. Being kind to others does that. It's contagious.

Every person on Earth has equal worth in God's eyes. No one is better than anyone else. The homeless person on the street is just as valuable as the most admired athlete, musician, businessperson, or movie star. However, in our society, athletes and actors appear to be more significant in some people's eyes simply because they're seen by millions on television, in the movies, or in magazines and newspapers. It's hard to stay humble when so many people put celebrities on a pedestal. After being worshiped for a while, it becomes "normal" for celebrities to think they're a step above the rest of the populace. And that's why they brush off fans who annoy them.

But the fact remains—we're all equal. Maybe you're not a famous person, but anyone can get caught up in the celebrity syndrome. Do you see others as unimportant or crowding your space? If so, you'll never be able to help them. The Bible says, "With humility of mind let each of you regard one another as more important than himself."[2] Even though no person is better, we are to *regard* others as more important. Rather than seeing others as our servants, we need to see ourselves as their servants.

I want to treat everyone I meet with dignity—because human beings are the most valuable of God's creation.

NEVER GIVE UP ON PEOPLE

I refuse to give up on people. Instead, I keep praying for them. I try always to remember that God can change anyone—if that person will look to Him. At one time, it looked like I was beyond help. But if God could save me, then He can save anyone. As long as a person is alive, there's still a chance that he or she might see the light and find the way.

Because my father was an alcoholic, my mother was forced to work two jobs to support us. The money my father earned as a railroad worker went toward buying liquor instead of food for the family. As a young man, I remember walking down the street one day, along with my friends, when I saw my father staggering around drunk. He wobbled a bit, teetered one way, then the next, and then passed out and fell into a ditch.

I was ashamed for my friends to see my father in that condition. My friends hadn't noticed him, so I quickly diverted their attention in another direction. After we arrived where we were going, I made a hasty exit. I told my friends, "Hey, I've got to go. See you later." Immediately, I ran back and pulled my father out of the ditch. No matter how many times our family had asked him to quit drinking, he couldn't stop. Like many alcoholics, he appeared to be beyond hope, and my mother separated from him because of his drinking problem.

SOMETIMES PEOPLE JUST NEED ONE MORE OPPORTUNITY TO PROVE THEMSELVES.

Years later, after I found God, I often went out on the streets and preached to pedestrians passing by. One day I preached on a street corner near the place where my father lived. It shocked him to hear me giving a sermon, but he listened intently to what I was telling everyone.

A few days later he told my mother, "Something's happened to George. I don't know what it is, but I want to find out." A week later, he started attending the church where I was preaching. My father eventually trusted Christ to save him, and the Lord miraculously set him free from his alcohol addiction. He never took another drink for the last twenty-plus years of his life. When I think about how the good Lord delivered my father, I am convinced that no one is beyond hope!

After his conversion, my father faithfully attended church each week. He even helped me whenever I'd go street preaching. I called him "Brother Foreman," and he referred to me as "Preacher." We became so close that it made my mother envious, so she started attending church, too. Before long, other family members also started coming to church. God's love is contagious!

Thanks to the Lord, my parents became the greatest of friends again. Before he died, my father told me, "Your mother is the only woman I've ever loved." She said something similar about him.

Never give up on people. As long as they're alive, there's still hope for change. If the Lord can change an alcoholic like my father and a hateful person like me, He can change anyone. Who knows? Maybe you're the one God wants to use to start the change within your family.

GIVE OTHERS ANOTHER CHANCE

Some people just need a chance to start over. My trainer in years past, Charley Shipes, got into trouble with the law and spent some time in prison. He was one of the men in the dressing room who had witnessed my encounter with God. Now he needed me to vouch for his parole.

That was awkward for me because I had never before helped someone in that type of situation. But the parole officers came to visit with me and asked if I would be willing to make sure Charley reported in on a regular basis. They hinted that I might be accountable if he jumped parole.

NO ONE IS BEYOND HOPE!

I knew I would be taking a risk if I vouched for Charley. As I was considering the situation, I asked my mother for her advice. She was usually suspicious of people's motives when they asked me to help them. But this time, she shocked me by supporting the idea.

"I know Charley," she said. "All he needs is another chance."

I'd never heard her say that about anyone. Usually she slammed down the judgment hammer on everyone—boom! But I knew what Charley needed: another chance to get his life straightened out, another chance to prove himself. I agreed to help him.

Whenever Charley went out of town, he checked with his parole officer. He always stayed straight and obeyed the law. He eventually got off parole and proved himself to be a model citizen. In fact, he later became a millionaire!

My mother's belief in him was the push I needed to help Charley succeed.

Maybe someone you know has messed up. You're afraid to give that person a second chance because you think he will take advantage of you. Not necessarily. If he or she is serious about changing, it will be worth taking the risk. Sometimes people just need one more opportunity to prove themselves.

And that's the way I look at people. God gave me another chance to live, so it has become my nature to give others a second chance, too. Sometimes it's not until later that I'll see the reward of helping a person.

Years ago, a college student called me, crying about losing his scholarship at UCLA. He asked if I could help him, so I sent him $1,000. Fifteen years later, he came to my house and repaid the $1,000. He had started his own business and wanted to hand me the money in person. He said, "I will never forget what you did for me!"

In 1983, one of the boys at the George Foreman Youth Center in Houston needed some hand wraps for boxing. The wraps cost $5, but he didn't have any money. I told him, "I'll give you the wraps, but as soon as you get the money, you need to pay back the $5. I want you to understand that nothing is free in life. Everything costs something."

He stayed in the program for a while, although he didn't pay back the money. Eventually, I lost track of him.

About ten years later, I drove into a full-service gas station in Houston. The attendant greeted me enthusiastically, pumped my gas, cleaned my windows, and then said, "Wait a minute. I'll be right back."

He hurried back and handed me a five-dollar bill.

I couldn't figure out why he would give me money to clean my windows. "What's this for?"

"Do you remember the hand wraps that you bought for me at the youth center a long time ago?" he asked. "I'm paying you back, just like you asked."

I took his money. That made him feel good, but it made me feel even better. That $5 was more important to me than the millions I've won in the boxing ring. It's one of my favorite memories of helping people.

Why? Because he was inspired to be a better person.

BE THE NICEST PERSON

I've told my children, "You might not be the tallest person in your school. You may not be the smartest, the most attractive, or the best athlete. But you can be the *nicest* person in your school."

I want to be known as the kindest human being on the planet. If someone tells me, "I've met a nicer person than George Foreman," then I'm going to find that individual and emulate whatever he or she is doing. That person will be my role model. I want to treat everyone as Jesus would. Even if someone is mean or rude to me, I will still be friendly to them. If I'm helping someone who tries to take advantage of me, I'll continue to assist him and then ask, "Is there anything else I can do for you?" I'm not going to be naïve, but I want to help others as best I can.

A man who was working for one of my neighbors—a man whom I had never met—came in my yard one day when I accidentally left my gate open. I was in the garage and didn't know he was on my property until he walked in. I wasn't sure of his intentions.

"Hey, George," he announced, "how are you doing? I have some hats that I want you to sign."

I could have reacted in anger and ordered him off my property. I could have said, "You've got some nerve coming in here! What are you doing trespassing on my property? I don't know you, so get out of here before I call the cops!"

But he wasn't hurting anyone. He wasn't there trying to rob me. He just wanted me to autograph some items for his family. So instead of blowing up, I shook his hand and introduced myself. "Hi, I'm George Foreman. It's so good to meet you." I wanted him to feel loved and accepted. I didn't want him to think that I was rejecting him or that he was unimportant.

He handed me a stack of hats, which I gladly signed for him. We visited for a while, and he gave me his business card. Even though it wasn't right for him to barge into my garage uninvited, I decided to be the nicest person he had ever met.

That's my calling in life—to invest my life in others. Nearly everyone goes through some kind of difficulty every day. A good dose of encouragement can be just what the doctor ordered. Sometimes the best way to encourage others is to just spend time with them and make them feel valued.

I started the George Foreman Youth Center to invest in future generations. The kids will come to the center to hang out and play basketball. They love it when I sit there and watch them play. It makes them feel special, if only for that day. Then I try to encourage them to come back. I'll say, "If you come next week, I'll watch you play again." Many of the kids do return so I can watch them play. They just need someone to notice them.

The next week they'll come back and bring a buddy with them. The friend will say, "You're right, man. You said George would be here to watch us." Kids need someone to take an interest in them, to pay attention to them, to help them feel like they're worth something. That's the encouragement they need. Then, years later, when they have kids of their own, hopefully they'll remember to give them attention, too. Maybe if I treat others with kindness, they will be inspired to pass it on.

PLANT SEEDS OF GREATNESS

When I was a small boy, my father planted a seed of greatness in my mind about my future. As we played, he often raised my hands over my head as if I had just won a boxing match, and he'd shout, "George Foreman, heavyweight champion of the world! Stronger than Jack Johnson. Hits like Jack Dempsey!" Even though I didn't understand what "heavyweight champion of the world" meant, he planted an idea in my mind that eventually became a reality.

It's incredible that he declared those things about me, almost like a prophecy about my future. It's even more amazing that I would not only become heavyweight champion, but also come back from retirement and win it a second time twenty years later. My father started proclaiming my destiny when I was only four years old and continued saying it until I was a teenager.

PARENTS NEED TO CORRECT THEIR CHILDREN, BUT THEY ALSO NEED TO MAKE AN EQUAL AMOUNT OF TIME TO ENCOURAGE THEM.

A parent's words can have a powerful influence in the life of a child. You can shape your children's destinies by speaking encouraging words about them, about who they are, not merely what they can do. Fathers who lived during the Old Testament days blessed their children concerning their futures. They believed their prophetic words would come to pass one day.

Just as those Old Testament patriarchs blessed their children, you can speak words of blessing to your kids as well. Speak encouraging words. Tell them, "You're going to do well in life. God has good plans for you. You are a champion!"

That doesn't mean you shouldn't speak words of correction. I have children, too, and it seems like I have to get after them about something every day. When kids do something wrong, parents have a responsibility to correct them. If your children don't do their best on their school work, or their room needs to be cleaned, or they're on the phone too long—that's when you need to put your foot down.

But always remember to apply an equal amount of time in encouraging them. Your children can remember home as a place where "they got on me about everything," or they can remember it as a place where "they always encouraged me." Kids who are encouraged by their parents usually turn out to be encouragers to others.

I want to make certain that my children think of our home as a place of encouragement. Yes, kids do have to be corrected and sometimes disciplined. But correction shouldn't be the most dominant thing they remember about growing up. They need to have memories of their parents supporting them. And they need to have a positive relationship with their parents if the correction and encouragement they receive are going to be effective.

Plant a seed of greatness in your children. Speak a word of encouragement to someone who needs to hear it. Inspire someone to be a better person. One day you'll reap a harvest, and your world will become a better place to live.

TIPS FROM GEORGE'S CORNER
ON INSPIRING OTHERS

- Treat everyone with dignity.
- Give someone who has failed another chance.
- Encourage someone who is going through a difficult time.
- Plant a seed of greatness in each of your children.

11
ADVANCING THROUGH ADVERSITY

NOT MANY PEOPLE HAVE TAKEN SUCH A CRAZY RIDE THROUGH life as I have. I'm probably one of those few people in the world who has gone from rags to riches to rags and back to riches again. Having grown up in extreme poverty, I became a millionaire, and then went bankrupt. Now I'm better off than ever.

The house I was born in didn't even have a bathroom. In 1957, we still used an outhouse. My lunch at school consisted of a mayonnaise sandwich and water from the drinking fountain. Then, after I became successful, I lived in houses all over the world, ate the finest foods at the nicest restaurants, and drove expensive cars. I earned over $10 million in the first phase of my boxing career. But I didn't know God at that time.

Even after becoming a believer, my troubles didn't completely disappear. In 1985, when I found out that my investors had lost most of my money and a business partner had drained my personal bank account, I was shocked!

I had been living under the illusion that I was financially secure for life. I suddenly came to the rude awakening that I was bankrupt.

After hearing the bad news, I remembered what the Bible said about Job when he lost everything. He said, "Naked I came from my mother's womb, and naked shall I return there. The LORD gave and the LORD has taken away, blessed be the name of the Lord."[1] I told God the same thing, shed a few tears, and then went about my business.

HOW MANY PEOPLE EXPECT THE FORMER HEAVYWEIGHT CHAMPION OF THE WORLD TO BE DIGGING THROUGH THE "DENTED CANS" BOX?

Was I upset that millions of my hard-earned dollars were gone? Of course! But I decided I wasn't going to let my problems depress me. Life is more than money. Nevertheless, the loss did dramatically affect my lifestyle.

One of the first things I had to change was how I shopped. When I was rich, I didn't need to be on a budget. I bought the best that money could buy and never considered the price. I couldn't do that anymore. I had to sell things that I owned just so I could buy groceries for my family.

As I pushed my shopping cart with the wobbly wheel down the grocery store aisles, I carefully searched for bargains. With so little cash in my pocket, I could only afford to buy the least expensive no-name brands.

I pulled boxes off the shelf that simply read "Detergent" instead of "Tide." I looked for generic toilet tissue instead of "Charmin." Before the good Lord cganged me, if someone had brought me an inexpensive, generic item, I would have been insulted. Now as I picked up each cut-rate product, I thanked God for the savings. Keep in mind, this is *after* I had been the boxing champion of the world! Now, because I had so little, I had a greater appreciation for simple things. I decided that my happiness wasn't going to be based on how much I owned, or how much I spent on laundry detergent or toilet tissue or any other material item.

My situation was particularly unusual when you consider how far I had fallen in terms of net worth—from the top of the mountain to the bottom of the valley. When I was the "old George," I went shopping for a Rolls Royce one day. When the salesman offered to knock off so many thousands of dollars, I was offended that he implied that a less expensive price tag might be a factor to me.

"What are you trying to do?" I said. "Do you think I don't have the money to buy this car?" I actually got mad when he tried to do me a favor. I wanted to pay the full sticker price! I didn't want to hear anything about a better deal.

When you're a celebrity, everyone is watching everything you do, and some people gawk at all the items in your shopping cart. When you're not famous, no one cares. Now that I was one of the "common folk," no one ever recognized me as I shopped. I didn't look the same as when I was boxing. It had been several years since I had retired, and my appearance had changed during that time. I had shaved my head and put on a lot of weight, so no one knew me. Besides, how many people expect the former heavyweight champion of the world to be digging through the discount racks or the "dented cans" box?

I HAD TO SELL THINGS THAT I OWNED JUST SO I COULD BUY GROCERIES.

But it didn't bother me to go bargain shopping. In fact, I actually enjoyed buying those discounted items with the rest of the poor people. I learned to be happy as a rich man, but I also learned to be content as a poor man. Even though I had lost everything, I could laugh louder than anyone in the room. I refused to allow circumstances to steal my joy.

No longer did I cruise around in my Rolls Royce. I bought an old car from a used car dealer and drove it to my relatives' house. They thought I was crazy for driving that clunker.

"George, you're so rich, you can buy anything you want. What are you doing driving that old car?"

I didn't tell them that I had gone bankrupt because I didn't want them worrying about me. I just gave them an ambiguous answer.

During this time, I was a full-time preacher with a small congregation. One Sunday I preached on God's faithfulness. I spoke from Psalm 37:25, which says, "I have been young, and now am old; yet I have not seen the righteous forsaken, nor his descendants begging bread."

Even though I was broke, I prayed, "Lord, you're not going to forsake me, and I'm not going to forsake preaching this message. This is the truth.

Nobody is ever going to make me say, 'This Bible is not true.' David said, 'I've *never* seen the righteous forsaken.'"

Even at that desperate time in my life, I knew God would supply all of my needs. I trusted the Lord to provide during my time of "famine."

My situation was similar to that of the widow in the Bible who was directed by God to feed the prophet Elijah; she obeyed God and her own bowl of flour never ran out. Her little jar of oil never became empty. Every time she looked in it, there was always more in that jar. That's what happened to me. Even today, now that I've regained my wealth, I don't view my bank account as a "big jar." I just see what I have as God's provision. He promised to take care of me.

WITH EVERY LEVEL OF ACHIEVEMENT COMES A NEW SET OF DIFFICULTIES.

And He has. Just like He blessed Job with twice as much, He did that and more for me. The Lord pulled me out of the pit and placed me back on a mountaintop higher than the first one. Since my bankruptcy, I've been blessed with greater wealth than ever before. By 1994 I had earned more than $50 million in boxing alone. That figure does not include the proceeds from my businesses.

God has proven Himself to me time and again. I've learned to trust in His faithfulness. I've learned that He's in control, even when things look out of control. Knowing that God was in my corner carried me through my times of adversity. He will do the same for you, too.

I FEEL YOUR PAIN

I've had to overcome a lot of adversity during my lifetime, and it didn't go away simply because I placed my trust in God. Some people think it is possible to go through life and never have a problem. They assume they must be doing something wrong when they experience a season of hardship. But trials are a part of life, even for a person who believes in God. Financial failures and people problems can cause a great amount of heartache and pain. I know they have for me.

The next time you attend a football game, take notice of the athlete who is limping or having an ice pack applied to his knee. It is obvious he has been competing in the game and has suffered pain as a result. Those who sit idly on the sidelines are missing out on the game experience. Often, the fact that the player is hurting means he's been giving it all he's got. He's not simply a spectator; he's actively participating in the sport.

When you feel pain, it means you're involved in the game of life. Adversity is a part of the contest; life would be boring without it. You don't want to be excluded from agony, because that would mean you were dead.

The lifeless bodies down at the county morgue don't ever feel pain. Have you ever heard them say, "Oh my, these bills are killing me!" When my mother passed away, the bills still came to her house, but she never said a word about them. Dead people don't holler about the debts they owe. Only when people are alive will they talk about their pain.

No person who is breathing can escape experiencing trials and tribulations. Being rich doesn't shield you from it. Being poor doesn't exempt you from it. Being famous doesn't protect you from it. You still have to wake up in the morning and say, "Here we go again." You'll have to learn to handle adversity whether you are at the bottom or at the top. With every level of achievement comes a new set of difficulties.

> **GOD IS IN CONTROL, EVEN WHEN THINGS LOOK OUT OF CONTROL.**

My friend Dave McMillan was born in Great Britain but came to America as boy, where he joined a circus. Dave became an expert lion and tiger trainer and eventually established himself as one of the top animal trainers in California. He and his wife were especially famous for their work training lions, tigers, and bears. Dave once helped train a lion and a tiger that I kept for a while on my own property. Needless to say, we didn't have any unexpected intruders during that time!

One night in the dead of winter 1979, I received a call from Dave; he was living in New Jersey at the time, and I could tell immediately that he was distraught. "My wife left me, George," he sobbed on the phone, "I don't know what to do. She doesn't want to come back to me. I just feel like giving up. I don't even want to live anymore."

I went to New Jersey and spent a few days with Dave, trying to encourage him. Before long, our conversation turned naturally to God and how He had helped me. "I think God can help you too, Dave," I told him, "if you'll just give Him a chance." I explained to my friend how he could have a relationship with God by believing in Jesus Christ.

"Tell me more about that baptism thing," Dave said when I told him that Jesus commanded us to repent—to turn around 180 degrees away from evil—and to be baptized. I explained that the place and method of baptism aren't the most important aspects since baptism is an outward symbol and expression of what has already happened in a person's heart. I told Dave how true believers in Jesus usually are baptized to show that one way of life is dead and buried and they have risen to a new life.

> **YOU CAN ALWAYS FIND SOMETHING POSITIVE IN EVERY NEGATIVE SITUATION.**

"Let's do it now," Dave said. "I have a swimming pool in the backyard. You can baptize me right there, can't you, George?"

"Now?" I asked. "It's freezing out there, Dave. There's ice in the water."

"But I'm a new believer, and that might help me, so I should be baptized right away, George."

"It's cold, Dave," I said, hoping I could talk him into waiting for a nice, warm opportunity to be baptized.

"Are you scared?"

"No, I'm not scared," I replied. "If you really want to do it, I'll baptize you right now." We went outside and pulled the cover off the shallow end of the swimming pool. Dave and I eased slowly into the water, and I put my arm around his shoulder. "Do you intend to live for Jesus all the days of your life?" I asked him, my teeth already chattering.

"Yes, I do," Dave answered.

Dave held on to my left arm as I used my right arm to lean him back beneath the cold water, baptizing him as a new believer in Jesus. When his head popped up out of the water, Dave was practically glowing. "George! I feel so fresh and clean on the inside," he cried.

"That's good!" I said. "Now let's get out of this freezing water and get warm." We went inside, and after we changed into dry clothes, Dave and I sat and talked for a long time about how he could trust the good Lord with every detail of his life, even the difficult issues surrounding his divorce. "Stay close to God," I said. "He'll never leave you or forsake you."

The next day, Dave said, "George, I know it isn't going to be easy, but I feel so good about life."

We stayed in touch for a number of years, and then our lives went in different directions. I hadn't heard from him for a long time when I received word informing me that Dave's son, Brandon, had died tragically.

I contacted Dave just to offer my condolences and to see if there was anything I could do to help.

Dave was crushed by the untimely death of his boy, but his faith in God was still strong. Dave spoke quietly but firmly into the phone "George, it's rough, but I've never lost my faith in the Lord. I tell people all the time about how you baptized me back there in New Jersey. You helped me establish a relationship with Him a long time ago, and I still have God. I've lost a lot in this life, but I've never lost God. He's been with me through it all, through the good times and the bad, each step of the way. Without Him, I don't know that I could make it through this. But I'm still serving the Lord."

Adversity touches all of us, but with the good Lord's help, we can make it through and come out stronger.

LOOK ON THE BRIGHT SIDE

Advancing through adversity requires a positive attitude. If you look closely enough, you can always find something positive in every negative situation. Optimism is in the eye of the beholder. Instead of looking at the minus side of your hardship, choose to look at the plus side.

Struggling actors long for the day when they become famous and have their pictures in all the magazines. But not long after they've reached celebrity status, they start resenting the very people who elevated them to that place. They detest the paparazzi whenever they snap a picture. If it weren't for the journalists, they wouldn't be famous! When fans ask for their autographs, the movie stars push them away. They can't stand being around the ones who admire them the most. Oh, the irony; at one time they craved being in the spotlight, and now they're running from cameras and hiding from the public!

An overwhelming amount of attention comes with celebrity status. It's part of the cost of fame. That popularity can be perceived in one of two ways—

as an invasion of privacy or as an honor because you are loved by so many fans. Every famous person chooses which way he or she will regard admirers.

Having been in the spotlight at times myself, I've learned to view popularity as a blessing. It's an honor to have people admire me so much that they'll follow me down the street to take a picture. It's a privilege to make others feel good just by signing my name for them. An autograph is just scribbling on a piece of paper, but that small gesture can make someone's day. The privilege that fame brings doesn't last forever. With time, the spotlight eventually moves off you and on to another. Then you become a *former* famous person, and that's not always an easy position to play.

I recently met with a college football player who had been drafted by the National Football League. Newspapers had been reporting that he hadn't done well on his Wonderlic Test, which the NFL uses to measure an athlete's intelligence. His rumored low test score was posted on numerous Internet Web sites and was being discussed in football forums and in chat rooms. Sports fanatics were saying that he would never make it in pro football, which bothered him.

"Don't let it get you down," I told him. "You should be celebrating! Pain means you're officially *in the game* now. You can't be successful without overcoming some adversity. This is the greatest time in your life. Everyone is talking about you. One day, maybe ten or twenty years from now, you'll wish that someone would snap some photographs of you like they're doing now.

"This is your time. Celebrate it. You should be happy they're talking about you. Learn to enjoy today in spite of the critics. Keep a smile on your face. Then when another player doesn't do well on that test, he'll remember how you handled the situation and that you didn't let it bother you."

Always look for the bright side of the situation. It's not always easy to find, but it's vital that you see it when you can.

STORMS DON'T LAST

Someone once asked an elderly woman her favorite Scripture verse. She replied, "And it came to pass."

"'And it came to pass?' But that doesn't mean anything."

"Yes, it does," she answered. "I know that whenever a trial comes, it doesn't come to stay; it comes—to pass. It's not going to be around forever."

It's wise to remember that our difficulties usually come in waves. At times, it seems like everything is crashing down around us, but then the tough time is followed by a period of peace. Sometimes the trial ends almost as quickly as it came. Keep trusting the Lord to take you through the storm.

One of the most difficult experiences of my life took place *after* I had been following the Lord for several years, when my wife at the time decided she no longer wanted to be married to the "new George." A sophisticated, well-educated woman, she had different goals and dreams, and being the wife

> **THE SEVERITY OF THE STORM HAD NOTHING TO DO WITH PETER'S ABILITY TO WALK ON WATER.**

of a poor preacher was not one of them. Increasingly, we found ourselves living in two different worlds with nearly opposite priorities. I knew our marriage was over before she said the words, but I was nonetheless shattered when I returned home after preaching one Sunday morning and found the house empty and all her clothes gone.

I was devastated, not simply because of my own sadness, but for the impact that my divorce might have on members of our church and others to whom I had preached. After all, I was the guy telling them that God could change any circumstances, that no problem between two people was irreconcilable when He was in the center, that He could turn their situations around for good if they would trust Him. Now here I was decimated by divorce and hanging on to hope by a thread.

Some of the toughest times were right there in church. I knew I had to get up on Sunday and put on a smile. People were depending on me to preach the truth, whether I felt like it or not. I'd do my best to get through the service, then I'd hurry to the car and weep all the way home. I honestly worried that I might go mad. During one excruciatingly painful point, I cried so loudly that I had to go into a closet to keep my neighbors from hearing me. I prayed, "Lord, if You will bring me through this, I will tell my story to everyone who has fallen into despair so they can lean on Jesus and receive hope."

By the next day, that huge weight lifted off me. It was over. It came to pass. Driving down the road, with tears filling my eyes, I said along with Job of old, "Though He slay me, yet will I trust Him."[2]

In times of crisis, release your burdens to the Lord in prayer. Keep your eyes on Him and not on the storm you're going through.

I love the biblical account in which the disciples were huddled together in a boat on the Sea of Galilee during a terrible storm when Jesus came walking to them on the water. Peter thought he'd like to do that too, so Jesus told him to get out of the boat. Peter walked on the water for a few steps, but then he took his eyes off Jesus. The moment he did that, he took an unexpected swim. He had lost faith because he focused on the storm going on around him rather than on the Lord.

> YOU MUST THINK HIGHER OF YOURSELF THAN WHAT YOUR DETRACTORS ARE SAYING ABOUT YOU.

But the severity of the storm had *nothing* to do with Peter's ability to walk on water. He never had the power to do it in the first place. Jesus gave him that capability. The storm was just a distraction to get him to look away from God.

If you're going through one of life's storms, keep your focus on the One who can help you—the good Lord. Don't get distracted by the loudness of the thunder, the flashing lightning, or the size of the waves. Remember, only God can give you the ability to "walk on water" in your life. Keep your eyes on Jesus and you'll supernaturally walk above your adversity.

WHEN OTHERS ATTACK YOU

Someone once told me, "No one spears a dead fish." It's only when you're alive that people will start throwing their spears. Criticism is part of the package that comes with success. I've seen movie stars crying because of the lies written about them in tabloids. Even if they receive an Academy Award, being smeared in a gossip magazine can steal their happiness before the Oscar is ever set on the fireplace mantel.

Don't let personal attacks on you determine how you feel. When you're on the bottom, people will treat you like you're on the bottom. But if you're on the bottom and *you see yourself on top*, their hateful comments won't bother you.

You must think higher of yourself than what your detractors are saying about you. If you're living on a higher level, when people try to hurt you, they're only hitting you on your ankles. I'm not talking about being proud; I mean that I choose to believe what God says about me over what anyone else might say.

When I'm being criticized, I try to rise above the derogatory or negative comments. For instance, when I climbed in the ring during my comeback, the announcers often introduced me as "the former heavyweight champion of the world." They were right in doing so, I suppose. But I refused to think of myself as the "former" champ; I focused on an image of myself as the current heavyweight champion, even though I hadn't actually won the title yet.

As they introduced me, I'd mumble to myself, "And the next heavyweight champion of the world."

How could I ever win the title if I didn't believe that I could? If you have a great dream you are attempting to fulfill in your life, you've got to believe it can happen before you can actually do it.

I wasn't trying to be proud. I simply believed what God had promised me—that I would regain the title. There's nothing wrong with that. While many people think too highly of themselves, many others think too lowly of themselves. They view themselves as worthless instead of as a valuable person God created and for whom Jesus died. You can't put a price tag on a person's worth.

When people said bad things about me, I thought, *They're just hitting me on my heels.* They weren't hitting me high enough to hurt. I wouldn't allow them to bring me down to their level, so how could they offend me? You can only be offended if you lower yourself down to the critics' standards.

> **YOU'VE GOT TO BELIEVE IT CAN HAPPEN BEFORE YOU CAN ACTUALLY DO IT.**

People can't hurt me with their comments when I know what God says about me. His opinion of me is what's most important, not what anyone else thinks. I threw myself on His mercy when I said, "God, I can't do it on my own. You'll have to do it through me." When I said that, the Lord gave me an inward strength that I didn't have on my own. If He did it for me, I know He can do the same thing for you.

When people attack you, don't lower yourself to their level. When they say things that aren't true, don't let it upset you. If you get offended, it gives the impression that what they say must be true. God doesn't want you to give their lies another thought.

Remember that trials are just a test to see what you really believe. The test is this: *Am I going to panic in my darkest hour? Or am I going to trust God to bring me through this?* The Lord will give you the strength to make it through your difficulty if you'll pray for His will to be done instead of yours.

Whatever the source of your trials, don't let adversity distract you. Why? Because you've got to press past the pain so you can get to where you're going.

TIPS FROM GEORGE'S CORNER
ON ADVANCING THROUGH ADVERSITY

- Trust God to control your situation.
- Look for something positive in your negative situation.
- Remember that trials "come to pass."
- Think higher of yourself than what your attackers are saying about you.

12

INTEGRITY—DON'T LEAVE HOME WITHOUT IT

INTEGRITY IS ONE OF THOSE WORDS WE THROW INTO A LOT OF conversations nowadays, but the definition often remains ambiguous. However we define it, I believe a person's integrity is only as good as his word. I've had numerous tests of my integrity, one in particular that could have cost me my second boxing career.

As I was working my way back up the heavyweight rankings, I was scheduled to fight in Atlantic City, New Jersey, the night before Mike Tyson was fighting Michael Spinks for the heavyweight championship of the world. The plan was to capitalize on all the media frenzy surrounding the Tyson bout, since the town was teeming with sports reporters and celebrities. I knew this boxing match could be a major stepping-stone toward where I wanted to go in my revived career, so I was looking forward to it.

But when I arrived in Atlantic City, I discovered that the promoters were not sticking to their word. In my contract, I had agreed to fight any one of three boxers the promoters chose, but the man they had selected, Carlos Hernandez, was not one of the agreed-upon boxers. At that time, Carlos was a fighter with a reputation for losing his temper in the ring, and he had a history of kicking and scrapping during a fight. He was not somebody I would have chosen to fight, and I let the promoters know about it.

Since the promoters had not specifically named any particular boxer in the contract, they felt that they were within their rights to pit me against Hernandez. They said, "It's either this guy or nothing. Either take it or leave it!"

This was a real dilemma for me. The arena was already booked, the publicity was out, and the media was involved in the event, so what should I do? On the one hand, this fight could jump-start my whole career; but on the other hand, if I let those promoters get away with taking advantage of me like that, it would set a dangerous precedent.

I fumed to Charley Shipes, my longtime trainer, about the problem. "Charley, this isn't right, and it makes me so mad, I'm tempted to pack up my clothes, walk out of here, go on back home, and forget about this fight."

Charley looked me in the eyes and said, "I know you are disappointed, George, but I think you should go ahead and fulfill your contract."

"But it's not right, Charley!" I vented.

"No, it's not right, George," Charley said calmly. "What they are doing is not fair, but just remember what you have always told me, 'Evil lurks where disappointment lodges.'"

Charley was quoting one of my favorite sayings—a truth that I felt the good Lord had taught me. He was feeding it back to me when I least wanted to hear it. But I knew he was right. "Evil lurks where disappointment lodges." If I walked away from the fight because of my disappointment, it could destroy everything that I had been working toward—not just as a boxer, but as a person. I realized that my integrity was on the line, so I went ahead with the fight.

The match proceeded much as expected, when I suddenly caught Hernandez with a powerful punch to the jaw, hitting him so hard that his mouthpiece flew out of his mouth and landed on the canvas. I saw what had happened and stepped back. I looked at the referee and pointed toward the mouthpiece. "Get his mouthpiece," I hollered.

"No!" the ref yelled back. "You fight."

"No, you get his mouthpiece," I repeated.

Carlos, the raging bull boxer, wasn't accustomed to anyone watching out for him. He pushed around the ref and lurched in front of me. "Just come on, man!" he bellowed. "Come on."

I boxed him to the end of the round, trying to avoid blows to his jaw until he could replace his mouthpiece. We continued the bout, and I won the fight by a knockout in the fourth round.

Besides the victory, at least two other positive things resulted from what started out for me as a negative situation—the boxing match that I had nearly walked away from. One, that boxer saw that I had been trying to help him by fighting to get his mouthpiece replaced rather than taking advantage of him, and it changed his boxing demeanor forever. He realized that boxing was a sport that didn't have to be hateful.

Second, as a result of the mouthpiece matter, boxing passed a new rule that said basically, when a boxer's mouthpiece comes out, the fight must stop long enough for the mouthpiece to be rinsed off and replaced—time is called, similar to an injury time-out in other sports. The rule change was a direct result of the fight I almost refused. Had I walked away from that fight, not only would it have been a blow to my integrity; it would have been a blow to the sport of boxing.

Our personal integrity touches every area of our lives, and one of the areas where it often shows up is in the area of sexual temptation. I must admit, before I committed my life to God, I operated from sheer selfishness and lust—I wanted what I wanted, when I wanted it—and I usually got what I wanted.

But after I had that experience in Puerto Rico, I wanted to please God, not just myself. My new attitude threw me out of sync with some of my former girlfriends. When I first returned from Puerto Rico, I stayed with my mother, but eventually I moved back to my own home. Most of my friends were still unaware that the old George had died and I was a new person on the inside, so they stopped by the house at all hours of the day and night.

One night I was in the shower when a beautiful young woman named Shawn showed up. I had pursued Shawn vigorously prior to my conversion, so you can imagine the temptation when the lovely young woman surprised me by stepping into the shower with me—stark naked.

In the past, I would have been thrilled, but things had changed. Without anyone preaching at me, something inside said, "No, this is not right." I stepped out of the shower, wrapped a large towel around me, and began to dry off. Shawn quickly followed, so I tossed her a towel, too.

"George, what's wrong?" she asked. "I thought you would be happy to see me."

"I am happy to see you, Shawn, but not like this." I clumsily tried my best to explain the spiritual transformation that had happened to me. "I've found peace with God," I told her, "and I want to do things right from now on." I was learning early on in my new life that no matter how close to God we get in this world, temptation never goes away completely; it simply changes appearances. Maintaining my integrity is a day-to-day deal.

IF YOUR HEART ISN'T PLUGGED INTO GOD, THE BEST YOU CAN DO IS FAKE A GODLY LIFE.

Nowadays, I frequently go out of town on business. Before I leave, I'll tell my wife Mary, "I will be the same man away from you as I am at home." Every time I go on a trip alone, I always take my wife with me—in my heart. When I pack my bags, I try to think about everything I'll need for my journey. The most important item that I can't forget to take with me is my integrity. I won't leave home without it.

Whenever I'm away, I call Mary every day to say how much I love her. People can feel when they are loved and when they aren't. Because Mary knows that I love God and her, she never has to worry about me being unfaithful.

How do *you* stay out of trouble? Does your spouse have to hire a private eye to follow you around twenty-four hours a day? Is that the only way you can keep from wandering—if you know someone is watching you? When you have integrity, you don't need a private eye constantly on your trail. If a private detective followed me around, all he could write in his notes would be, "I don't have anything to report!"

The only one who truly knows everything you do is God. He reads every thought in your mind and analyzes every motive of your heart. Integrity means that you live right—not because a private eye is following you, but because you want to please God. You stand up for truth. You make right choices. You're honest in your business deals. You're the same person in private as what the public sees.

Our moral character is directly tied to our relationship with God. You don't get integrity by simply "trying to be good." But God can give you the power to live the way He wants and to help you stay on the right track.

When your heart is connected with God's heart, He will inject His character into you like a blood transfusion gives life to a patient. When you walk with the Lord, He will manifest His life *through* you. But if your heart isn't plugged into God, the best you can do is fake a godly life. You'll act one way in front of people and then be a totally different person in private.

That's like playing golf and keeping your own score. After each hole, you write down a lower score so you can win. Then you show everyone your scorecard and brag about shooting 70. But you must live with the knowledge you really shot 105. How satisfying is *that*?

You might get away with playing like you are godly for a while, but eventually you'll be discovered. Sooner or later people will figure out your performance doesn't match your scorecard. You can hide things from your neighbor, but what can you hide from God? Nothing. He sees everything you do. You're not fooling Him.

God gave me a second chance at life, and I'm determined to live it right this time. I've decided in my heart that I'm not going to live immorally like I did before. When my life is over, I don't want to look back and be sorry for the way I lived. I want God to say, "George, I gave you another chance, and you lived exactly like I wanted."

THE DOORS OF TEMPTATION

What is the secret to living with integrity? For one thing, my desire to please God must be stronger than the pull of temptation. When I died in 1977, I went to that terrifying, dark place. The foul odor was worse than anything I've smelled on Earth. Every morning when I get out of bed, I remember that rotten smell of death. I have flashbacks of being in that void of total darkness.

Can you imagine what it has been like for me to think about that place every single day for the last thirty years? The constant, daily reminder nullifies the lure of temptation for me. I never ever want to go back there. I don't want to be in that position again. It haunts me every day, every hour, every minute of my life. But it also keeps me in touch with God and helps me say no to temptation.

Most temptations come to you through certain doors you willingly open. That "door" could be a raunchy Web site on the Internet, a television program with degrading content, a business deal that isn't quite on the up-and-up, a magazine filled with lewd pictures, a substance that will harm your body, a person of bad influence, or a place where you know you shouldn't be. The answer is to stop the temptation *before* it can influence you.

> **YOU MUST MAKE THAT COVENANT WITH YOUR EYES BEFORE THE TEMPTATION COMES YOUR WAY.**

If you keep the door of temptation closed, it can't affect you. And if it can't affect you, it loses its power to influence you to do wrong. Way back in the beginning of the Bible, Cain killed his brother Abel because sin was crouching at the door, and Cain opened it.[1] That's why you can't give the devil an opportunity, because if you do, he'll come storming through the door. But you will reduce your temptations significantly if you'll just keep the door shut, or shut it quickly when temptation approaches.

That door could be a former lover. You must firmly shut the door forever on previous immoral relationships. Don't leave that door open, not even an inch. After you're married, one of the wisest steps you can take is to break off the communication lines and stop talking to former girlfriends or boyfriends unless your conversation is in the presence of your spouse. The doors of temptation are different for everybody, but learn a lesson from Adam and Eve: Don't go inspecting the tree looking for forbidden fruit. Stay away from it!

In the Bible, the man Job said, "I have made a covenant with my eyes; why then should I look upon a young woman?"[2] He was talking about lusting after someone who wasn't his wife.

He told his eyes, "Don't you go wandering after women, or I'll pluck you out!"

His eyes replied, "We see . . . and we want to keep on seeing."

Your eyes can get you into all kinds of trouble, so make them behave. Make that covenant with your eyes *before* the temptation comes your way. It's your heart that makes that agreement with your eyes. If your heart isn't connected to God's heart, there's no telling what kind of agreement you'll make. Notice, your personal integrity goes back to your relationship with God.

If Job were alive today, I doubt you'd find him going to a porn site on the Internet, buying a sleazy magazine, or watching X-rated movies. It wouldn't be because he was some kind of prude or a super human who was above temptation. God gave Job a strong sex drive, as evidenced by his wife's bearing numerous children. But he didn't try to fulfill his needs outside the boundaries of marriage. He kept his drive under control because he had made a covenant with his eyes—he closed them when he needed to and diverted his attention from anything that might cause him to compromise his commitment to God or his family.

> YOUR DESIRE TO PLEASE GOD MUST BE STRONGER THAN THE PULL OF TEMPTATION.

I've discovered that I can close my eyes to temptation too. Granted, temptation touches everyone—Jesus Himself was tempted, so you can be sure that you and I will be tempted in various ways. But if we learn to keep the door shut, or to shut it quickly when we recognize temptation's knock, we can avoid a lot of trouble.

NO COMPROMISE

I'm not going to lower my standards to get what I want. Lying, cheating, and stealing have to be evicted from my life if I'm going to live honestly and stand up for the truth. I will not compromise my convictions just so I will profit or win. I want to be able to look at myself in the mirror and not be ashamed.

When I previously boxed as the "old George," I was like a mean robot who wanted to kill people. I showed no mercy. Sometimes when I knocked down an opponent, as he was falling, I would punch him again before he hit the canvas. I was that vicious.

In one fight, when I hit my opponent as he was going down, his manager yelled to the referee, "Disqualify George! I'll give you $100,000 right now if you'll disqualify him!"

I'll admit that I was wrong to hit him again, and I could have been disqualified for it. But my opponent's manager was openly trying to bribe the referee. He possessed no better scruples than I did.

Before I met the Lord, compromising didn't bother me. Just before I fought Ali in Africa, my manager told me, "We need $25,000 to give the referee."

"Why?" I asked.

"So he doesn't disqualify you. He's not going to help you win, but the money will keep him from disqualifying you."

A referee can disqualify a boxer at his own discretion for just about anything, such as hitting below the belt or punching the other boxer when he's down. A ref usually just gives a warning, but he can also declare the fight over—and the other guy the winner. Since I was known to hit opponents as they were going down, I figured the ref wanted "assurance" money so I wouldn't have to worry about being disqualified. I gave him the money.

I WANT TO BE ABLE TO LOOK AT MYSELF IN THE MIRROR AND NOT BE ASHAMED.

I fought a clean fight and didn't do anything that would have disqualified me, so I needlessly flushed $25,000 down the drain. But when Ali knocked me down, the ref fast-counted me. When I stood up at the count of eight, he said "eight-nine-ten" as one word.

Later, in a *Sports Illustrated* interview, I admitted to giving the money to the referee. Awhile after that, I ran into Ali's former manager, who had read the article, along with his associate.

The ex-manager asked, "George, did you really give $25,000 to the ref?"

"Yep," I said, "so he wouldn't disqualify me."

His associate turned to him and asked, "How much did we pay him? Wasn't it $35,000?" The manager walked away without saying a word.

As I've already said, I'm happy I lost that fight to Ali because it was part of God's plan for me. But I tell that story to show my lack of integrity before I gave my life to the Lord Jesus.

God had to change my heart before I could live right—or even fight right! I couldn't take the old George with me on my new journey. When I knocked out Joe Frazier to win the heavyweight title for the first time, the old George made it a big celebration. He bragged about being the world's champion. He was so proud of himself. *Look what I did!*

That old fella had to die because he wouldn't fit inside the new George Foreman. I didn't try to prolong his days by keeping him on life support. I let him pass away, along with all his selfish hopes and dreams. After God changed my life, the new George didn't behave the same way. The old George bragged about how great he was, but the new George brags about how great God is.

When I returned to boxing in 1987, I did a lot of things differently than before. I wanted to be the heavyweight champion of the world, but I wasn't going to do it by paying off the judges or bribing the referee. If I couldn't win the title fair and square, I didn't want it. I wasn't going to pull any cheap tricks or do anything under the table anymore.

I live with a clear conscience. That's worth everything to me. It's not winning that counts. It's integrity.

SETTING A GOOD EXAMPLE

People are watching you. You can be a positive or a negative influence on them, depending on what kind of example you choose to be. In 1994, an opportunity came for me to have my own television sitcom called *George*, in which I played the lead character. Television star turned producer Tony Danza had approached me about doing a show in which I played a former champion who had a large family and spent most of his time helping kids. *Hey, I can play that part!* I thought. Now that I had Jesus Christ in my life, I wanted the show to be clean and fun for the whole family to watch. I soon found out that not everyone on the set shared that idea.

Every week when we received our scripts, they usually contained some crude jokes and off-color insinuations. As I read my part, I knew our staff would struggle between going along with the questionable humor or taking a stand for a more wholesome brand of humor. For me, it was an easy choice. I wasn't going to compromise my standards just so I could fit in the

Hollywood scene. I refused to let a desire for acceptance turn me into a person I didn't want to be.

The writers and the director and I met every Monday to go over the script, and inevitably, I had to ask them to clean it up with a rewrite. In one script, a tough kid was expected to say, "You don't want to make Shasta mad. If you make her mad, it would be like . . ." (crude humor).

Everyone on the set laughed—everyone, that is, except me. I told the producers and directors, "We're taking that line out."

They said, "No, that's funny. Everybody says that."

"I know some people think that's funny, but I don't want it said on my show. Millions of people are going to be watching. The viewers are allowing me to come into their living rooms every week because they trust the content of this show. We're not going to say that."

The writers took it out and changed the script. It would have been easy for me to simply go along with them, but I wanted the show to be a clean comedy for families. I didn't want anyone to remember me as using offensive humor on television. I want to be above reproach with everyone.

After I won the heavyweight championship the second time, everyone was celebrating and drinking champagne, but I never took one sip. Someone said, "George, you're the champ now. Aren't you going to celebrate?"

"You bet I'm going to celebrate," I said. "I'm going to drink this bottle of water and then catch a flight back to Houston. I've got to get back to my church and tell my congregation what happened tonight!"

"DELAYED GRATIFICATION" MEANS YOU'LL SAY NO TO AN ATTRACTION NOW TO RECEIVE SOMETHING BETTER LATER.

And that's how I celebrated winning the championship. By flying home and preaching about God's faithfulness in my church the next morning.

Integrity should cover every area of your life. People are watching what you do and listening to everything you say. I know people who will pull out a cigarette and ask, "Do you mind if I smoke?" But I've never heard anyone ask, "Do you mind if I cuss?" You can't ask to be seated in a cursing or noncursing section at a restaurant. You can pollute the air with words just like you can with smoke. Although a person's health can be ruined by inhaling secondhand smoke, his soul can be devastated if he hears cutting remarks about himself or someone else.

You might say, "George, I don't use curse words." Although you might not use *cuss*words, you can speak *curse* words if you gossip about someone or tell your kids they'll never amount to anything. That's putting a curse on them. Think how many adults still carry wounds from their childhoods because a parent spoke cruel words in a moment of anger.

When you walk in integrity, you're constantly aware of how you're influencing other people. I want my influence to be a good one.

DELAYED GRATIFICATION

Another key to maintaining integrity is to decide, "Am I an 'instant gratification' or a 'delayed gratification' person?" The instant gratification person has to have the Cadillac in the showroom window: "I've got to have it right now!" The delayed gratification person says, "I can't afford that right now, so I'm walking away from it." The day may come when he buys it, but he's not ruled by how he feels at that moment.

"Delayed gratification" means you'll say no to an attraction now to receive something better later. You're not going to give up what's important to you—whether it's virginity, marriage, or self-respect—in exchange for something you'll regret later.

To walk in integrity, I've learned to be a delayed gratification person. I can't sneak some forbidden fruit just because it looks good at the moment. When I encounter a potentially compromising situation, I'll turn and walk away because I understand the harm of yielding and the rewards of waiting. Although I might not get what I want right now, God will give me something better later, and it will be exactly what I need. The Lord has His own ways and time for rewarding His people.

However, without integrity, you'll take what you can get now rather than later, and you'll usually compromise your character to get it. But you should keep in mind that the forbidden fruit never tastes as sweet as it looks. And the Cadillac in the showcase window? It rusts! You'll find out that it wasn't worth the price you paid. Cheating never works because you can't fool God, and you can't fool yourself—although a lot of people try.

I heard someone say, "A man can stoop so low that it gets into his genes." That's true. A dishonest person can pass his deceitful ways down to his children. And so his instant gratification effects not only him, but also future generations.

In contrast, God makes an incredible promise to those who keep their integrity: "No good thing will He withhold from those who walk uprightly."[3] That's quite a promise! God will make sure that you receive every good thing you need, if you'll do what He says.

God pays special attention to those who live to please Him. When you live right, He blesses you, which makes life fulfilling and meaningful. People want to be happy, but sometimes they're just looking in the wrong places. If everyone truly understood the rewards for living honorably, they would never hesitate to do what is right.

Integrity is an investment of your life that is guaranteed to be rewarded both now and in the future. In my short time on Earth, I want my life to be a godly example that my kids will choose to follow. God even promises to pass the reward down to the next generation: "The righteous man walks in his integrity; his children are blessed after him."[4]

That's important to understand. Perhaps you're a parent who is doing everything right, but your children are rebelling. Maybe your kids are on drugs or are involved in immorality. You need to trust God's promise that He won't let go of them for *your* sake. So keep following God and praying for your children. They'll come back one day. And then you'll be able to say, "My kids *used to be* on drugs, but they aren't anymore. They're serving God!"

Although you might not see the profits of living wisely right now, the benefits will show up later. It may be that God will reward your faithfulness by blessing your children in an unusual way. Maybe the Lord will give your child great insights, and he or she will become a successful author, painter, or inventor. Or maybe your children will do something more "ordinary." That's okay, too. Regardless, to see your kids serving God is the greatest reward you can hope for this side of heaven.

Whether you're packing for a long trip or just making a trip to the grocery store, I hope you'll take your integrity with you. Keep it on you all the time, and don't leave home without it.

TIPS FROM GEORGE'S CORNER
ON HAVING INTEGRITY

- Connect your heart with God's heart by drawing close to Him.
- Prevent temptations by keeping the doors to compromise closed.
- Make a covenant with your eyes before temptation comes your way.

13
WHEN OPPORTUNITY KNOCKS, ANSWER THE DOOR

WHEN TEMPTATION KNOCKS ON THE DOOR, I KEEP IT CLOSED. BUT when opportunity knocks, I throw the door wide open! Opportunity doesn't knock nearly as often as temptation, so it is important to be ready when it comes calling. Unfortunately, many people let opportunities slip away because their fear of the unknown prevents them from opening the door.

With every new opportunity usually come adjustments that make people uncomfortable. Just mention the word "change," and then watch everyone panic! They'll tell you ten reasons why the new idea will never work. Most people feel safe inside their comfort zones and prefer to keep doing the same things over and over. It petrifies them to take a chance on anything.

And that's why they miss opportunity when it knocks. They're afraid of how their lives might change as a result. *If I take this risk, something bad might happen to me. Things will never be the same again.*

But a change in their routine is probably the thing they need the most. They're slowly dying inside because of boredom and are missing an exciting adventure that would make life better for them. Instead of seizing the opportunity, they give in to their fears. Fear always hitchhikes along with opportunity, trying to keep people from reaching their destinies.

When God is leading me, I don't worry about moving in a new or uncomfortable direction. Why should I be afraid when God is watching over me? Even though I may be exploring new territory, I don't need to be overly concerned because I know the Lord will give me strength and confidence.

I HAVE TO BE WILLING TO TRADE WHAT I HAVE FOR SOMETHING BETTER IN RETURN.

You'll probably change directions a number of times during your life, perhaps starting a new business, moving to a new town, or entering a new relationship. God will give you the strength you need to meet whatever challenges you'll face along the way. The "God factor" neutralizes the "fear factor." Just always be sure that wherever you go, you are following the True Leader, our good God.

Even when fear is not a factor, you might be surprised at how many people will try to discourage you from doing what God wants you to do. Whenever I told people that I was thinking about becoming a preacher, they looked at me funny and asked, "Why do you want to do *that*?" No one ever told me, "George, that's a great idea! You will touch a lot of lives and help a lot of people." But I refused to let their lack of enthusiasm keep me from fulfilling my calling. I seized my opportunity and "stepped into the ring."

COUNTING THE COST

Whenever I decide to make a change, I'm also making an exchange. I have to be willing to trade what I have for something better in return. That's why Jesus said to count the cost before making a decision. The cost is my initial investment—what I'll lose at first.

Let's say I have an opportunity to build a fifteen-story condominium. I'll need to figure the entire cost before I break ground. Otherwise, if I don't have enough money, I'll only build five stories and then have to quit. Then I've lost both my investment and the condo.

When I decided to return to boxing after not having fought for ten years, I had a price to pay. Opportunity brings change, which isn't easy. My goal was to be the champion again, and I knew to win the title would require enormous effort and sacrifice on my part.

I had to change the way I ate. Put the fork and spoon down sooner. No more fatty foods and ice cream. I couldn't sleep as long. I had to exercise and get back into shape. Because I was still the pastor of our church, I had to set my alarm two or three hours earlier so I could run and train before I went to work at the church office.

Would I have been happier sleeping later every morning, eating all those fattening foods, and not working so hard? Sure, the easy way can be enjoyable—for a while. But would I have been ready to compete for a championship? Not a chance.

Sometimes the people closest to you will try to stop you because your decision is going to affect them also. It's the domino effect—when you accept a new assignment and make a change, your family is forced to make adjustments, too. And that's a good reason why your spouse needs to be in agreement with you about the opportunity you are pursuing.

At first, my wife resisted and said, "George, if you go back into boxing, you're going to get killed." She later admitted that wasn't her only fear. She was also afraid that I would turn into the old, mean George—the way I used to be before I met Jesus. I needed her support, and she eventually agreed that boxing was what I should do. She had nothing to worry about; I didn't get killed, and I didn't turn into the old George.

One night I took my family to the theater to see a movie, and we had a great time together. My oldest

THE "GOD FACTOR" NEUTRALIZES THE "FEAR FACTOR."

daughter said, "You see, Dad, we had a good time at the movies and no one bothered us. If you go back to boxing, you'll never be able to do this again."

She was right. Things would change if I started boxing again. The chance to become champion again was a great opportunity, but we'd have to give up our family's privacy as part of the cost. Later when we would go to the movies, I had to make time to sign autographs, meet people, and chat. I couldn't go around unnoticed anymore. But God was leading me to return to boxing, and I wanted to go back. It was a fire burning in my heart.

When God leads you to make a change, it is not always easy, but it is always for the best. I understood that seizing this opportunity would affect everything in my life, but I was willing to take that chance. I knew my life would be different because I had already experienced being a champion. Because I counted the cost, I anticipated the challenges that lay ahead. I adapted my lifestyle, so the adjustments didn't bother me. Losing our privacy would happen again, just like before, but I knew better how to handle that pressure.

Looking back, it was well worth taking the risk. The rewards have been far greater than the sacrifices. But I shudder to think what life would be like now if I had been too afraid to answer the door when opportunity knocked.

MORE DOORS BEHIND THE FIRST DOOR

You may not realize initially how many other opportunities are wrapped up inside the first one. After you go through the first door, you'll then discover more doors automatically opening behind that one. One door leads you to another door, which leads to another door, and so on. It's like ten other boxes packed inside one box—the initial door that God opens is your access to more opportunities. But you must be willing to walk through the first one to get to the other good things God has for you.

Consider my opportunity to reenter boxing: Going through that initial door didn't just take me to the championship but also led to other opportunities such as doing commercials and a television show, being a boxing commentator, writing books, promoting the George Foreman Grill, and undertaking numerous other business ventures. None of that would have happened if I hadn't taken the first step. I had to be willing to take a risk.

You might be considering an opportunity at this very moment. If God is leading you, then dare to take a step of faith. You must be willing to take a chance. But you can't confidently walk through any door unless you've put your trust in the Lord. You must believe that God is leading you, and He won't let you down.

In 1986, God told me while I was praying that I would be doing television commercials one day. This was long before anyone had approached me to represent their product or company. The Lord said, "You will do well, because you will be promoting products with honesty."

A few years later, while I was making my comeback, I was sitting at home when the telephone rang. The caller said, "We're trying to find George Foreman."

Since I wasn't sure of his intentions, I asked, "May I ask why you need to talk to George Foreman?"

"We're trying to put a commercial together and want to talk to him about it."

"Oh! This is George!"

"Are you really George Foreman, the boxer?" he asked.

"Yes, this is George Foreman, the boxer."

"Great, I'm glad I found you! Nike is making a shoe commercial and wants you to be in it."

"A shoe commercial? Really?" I had never been in a commercial before. This was my second door of opportunity, which would not have happened if I hadn't gone through the first door.

"It's not much money," he continued, "but it won't take a lot of your time either."

I had been broke and wasn't making much money at this point in my comeback. I thought, *You don't know what "not much money" means. Five dollars is a lot of money to me!*

"Sure," I said, "I'll be glad to work with you."

So I did the commercial with pro football running back Bo Jackson. Bo was already a household name because of his "Bo knows" commercials, and Nike was looking for a fresh angle in using Bo Jackson. In the spot, some reporters asked Bo several questions about running. Since Bo knows everything about everything, they expected him to answer all their questions. Pretending to be irritated, he said, "Look, I don't have time for all this stuff!"

Just then, I jumped out of nowhere and said, "But I do!" And then I

> **AFTER YOU GO THROUGH THE FIRST DOOR, YOU'LL THEN DISCOVER MORE DOORS BEHIND THAT ONE.**

started dancing across the floor. The point was that the young athlete was too tired, but the forty-year-old "retired" athlete was full of energy and still wanted to make things happen (with the help of Nike products, of course). We had a lot of fun shooting the commercial, and it really connected with the public. People loved it and started calling out my name everywhere I went. "Hey, George! I saw you on the commercial with Bo."

Then a third door opened. The Nike commercial led to a McDonald's commercial. Everyone knew I liked to eat cheeseburgers, so a reporter asked me to rank all the hamburger restaurants from 1 to 10. When I graded the burgers, I didn't rank McDonald's as high as some of the others. Not to be outdone, McDonald's created a "George Foreman burger," which I promoted on television. In return, McDonald's donated an electronic scoreboard for my youth center.

Then I did a commercial with Doritos. After that, Oscar Mayer wieners. Then Kentucky Fried Chicken. In a Motel 6 commercial, I popped out of a suitcase. I've done ads for Meineke Car Care, Casual Male Big & Tall clothes, the George Foreman Knock-Out industrial cleaners, and one of my most successful ventures, the George Foreman Grill.

THE GEORGE FOREMAN GRILL STORY

I've learned not to discount an opportunity just because it doesn't pique my imagination or look too exciting at first. Sometimes all sorts of blessings are right behind an unopened door, but you'll never know if you don't open it.

A business friend came to me with an offer. He said, "George, you've helped other companies by advertising their products. Have you ever thought about having your own product?" Later he sent me a small, slanted grill and asked me to try it out.

I got busy with other things and forgot about it. A couple of months later, he called. "George, how do you like the grill?"

"Oh, the grill. To be honest, I haven't tried it yet. Let me get back with you on that."

After hanging up, I almost made one of the worst financial decisions I could ever make. I thought, *I really don't have time for this.*

Fortunately, Mary changed my mind. "George, I've tried the grill and I like it a lot. The grease rolls right off and the food tastes really good."

"Are you serious?"

"Yeah," she replied. "I'll fix you a burger."

After taking a bite, I said, "Yeah, it is really good. And the grill is easy to clean up. I like this grill!"

I wasn't thinking about making any money on the deal. I just signed the contract so I could get sixteen free grills for my homes, friends, and family members. I never dreamed this opportunity would turn into a grilling empire!

I ALMOST MADE ONE OF THE WORST FINANCIAL DECISIONS I COULD EVER MAKE.

After I made the first commercial to advertise the grill, sales skyrocketed. We were ecstatic when we sold one million grills. Then sales hit five million. Soon, ten million grills sold. It became so popular that Salton, the appliance maker, offered to pay me a fortune for my part of the George Foreman Grill.

Today, more than eighty million George Foreman grills have been sold worldwide. It won't be long before sales skyrocket past the hundred million mark. And it all started when a friend asked me to consider an interesting opportunity.

I give my wife, Mary, credit for the success of the George Foreman Grill because she was the first one to use the product and she sold *me* on it. I'm glad I listened to her. That one decision blessed not only my life, but also millions of others. You never know how making one small decision can change so many lives.

So many people were calling me to do commercials that I had to start saying no to them. When Oscar Mayer called, I asked them why they wanted me.

They said, "George, while we were writing this commercial, we asked around about who would be a good person to feature in the spot. Someone spoke up and said, 'Have you heard how George Foreman is working with kids in Houston? He started a youth center for them. Let's ask him to do the commercial.'"

One reason I started boxing again was to help pay for the youth center, and now the youth center was paying me back with the commercial. That's another example of how going through one door opened another opportunity.

I've worked with Meineke Car Center for many years. Most advertisers will only sign athletes to a one-year contract. It's the fear of association. Many companies don't want to be associated with someone too long. They're worried that the spokesperson might get involved in a scandal or that an athlete will lose his or her popularity.

But Meineke took a strong interest in me, and they've kept me as their spokesman since 1992. I've always had a great relationship with them. Products are sold on trust, and I won't endorse a product that I don't believe in.

I believe I've experienced every one of those business and professional opportunities because of the prayer I said years before: "God, if You can do something with my life, take it and use it." I'd encourage you to pray something similar, because God has a master plan for everyone. Carl Hempe wasn't extremely famous, but he smiled when he heard that God had used him to touch my life. I want to have that same smile on my face, knowing that God used me to positively influence other people's lives.

WALK AWAY FROM WRONG OPPORTUNITIES

Always use wisdom when you're considering a chance to move up. Sometimes an opportunity looks good, but you know something's not quite right about it. You can't explain why the reticence exists, but you get an unsettled feeling in your heart or mind as you ponder the possibility. Maybe it's the timing or the conditions that are attached to it. Regardless, if it doesn't feel right inside, be willing to walk away from it and wait for the Lord to open the right door in His timing. I'm not saying that stepping into a new season is easy, but if you don't have a sense of peace in the midst of the nervousness and excitement, I'd slow down and ask God for further directions. Nevertheless, don't be afraid to do things differently.

When I started boxing again, nobody wanted to promote boxing matches around the holidays. The ratings normally drop during the Thanksgiving and Christmas holiday season because people are shopping, traveling, and spending time with their families. But I decided to do something different. I called Bob Arum, the boxing promoter, and asked if he would schedule me for a match during that time period.

He was reluctant at first but finally said, "Okay, George. I won't do a multi-package deal, but I'll let you fight one time. We don't have much money. All I can pay you is $12,500."

"Okay, it's a deal—$12,500," I said, smiling on my end of the phone.

So I fought during the holiday season, when no one was supposed to be interested. To everyone's amazement, the Las Vegas arena filled to capacity, and the match received better ratings than any other ESPN boxing show on the air at that time. Bob Arum was shocked.

He came back to me and said, "George, I'd like to promote another fight for you. This time I'll pay you $100,000—but you have to fight one of the guys on my list." He showed me a list of highly ranked fighters.

"Sorry, Bob, but I'm not going to fight any of those guys at this time. They're too tough, and I'm not ready for them yet."

"But I was thinking about signing you to a multi-fight package," he explained.

"I never asked for that. Besides, you told me you didn't want to do that."

Bob got mad. "You've got to fight somebody. You can't fight those tomato cans forever!" He was talking about second-rate opponents who bleed easily.

I said, "Well, they aren't tomato cans to me. Some of those guys can really box, and they are all tough competitors who want to make a name for themselves by beating a heavyweight champion."

Since Bob and I couldn't reach an agreement, I turned down the money and walked away from the deal. Bob meant well, no doubt, but for me, it was a case of a wrong opportunity presenting itself, and I refused to take the bait. If I had fought any of those guys before I was ready for them, I would have lost. My comeback could have ended right then and there. But I knew if I'd be patient, the right opportunity would come knocking in God's timing.

Later, I picked up the sports page and read what Bob had told a sportswriter: "George Foreman doesn't want to fight anybody. He'll never be champion. He's too old."

I smiled; I think Bob may have said that to entice me to sign a deal with him. But I didn't. I kept fighting the less prominent opponents, getting stronger and more confident with each bout and slowly working my way up the rankings. When the USA network televised my fights, they had such good ratings that Bob Arum decided to contact me again. Although he had belittled me in the media, I never retaliated against him. Bob thought I might be angry with him, so he cautiously approached me.

"Hi, George. Uh, can I talk to you for a minute?"

I tried to ease the tension. "Sure, Bob, you can always talk to me."

"I have a proposition for you, and I think you'll like it."

> TOO MANY PEOPLE ARE REACHING FOR THE STARS AND FORGETTING ABOUT THE CHURCH.

This time he made me an offer that I could agree with—and it was for millions of dollars! By turning down the wrong opportunity and waiting for the right one, God gave me something much better.

Although the opportunities that come your way will be different from mine, you can follow the same principle: If something isn't right, be willing to turn it down and walk away.

MY FUTURE GOALS

I often tell people that I'm the "eighth wonder of the world." I received my first punch in the '40s when the doctor slapped my behind.

I threw my first punches in the '50s.

I won an Olympic gold medal in the '60s.

I became the heavyweight boxing champion of the world in the '70s.

In the '80s, I made every sports writer eat his words when I came back into boxing.

In the '90s, I stunned the sports world by winning the heavyweight championship of the world again.

Now, in the new millennium, I'm the king of the lean, mean, fat-burning George Foreman grilling machine!

I've spent more time in the George Foreman Grill business than I did in my second career in boxing. Although I won't be champ again in the ring, I'd like to be a champion in the business world. They called me "the King of the Grills" in 2005. I'd like to add to that and be the king of another new venture in the future.

Although I love sports and business, my real heart is for evangelism, sharing the good news with people about how they can find a genuine relationship with God. I speak as often as I can in churches around the country. I want to touch hearts for God. People need to understand that God is good and that His plan for us is good, not evil. He loves us more than we realize. We matter to God—to Him, we all are valuable, no matter if we have fame, fortune, or titles.

Ebony magazine came to Houston to interview me and took photos of me standing in front of my church. I told them my goal was to be preaching at that same church ten years from now. I want to be faithful with the opportunity that God has given me to serve Him as a pastor.

Too many people are reaching for the stars and forgetting about the church. Don't let any opportunity lead you away from serving God. That's a price that's too high to pay.

TIPS FROM GEORGE'S CORNER
ON SEIZING OPPORTUNITIES

- Don't let fear keep you from reaching your destiny.
- Consider what you'll have to give up, and what you'll get in return.
- Remember that going through one door usually opens other doors.
- Refuse any opportunity that leads you away from God.

14

THE SECRET OF SUCCESS

JOHNNY CARSON, THE FORMER HOST OF NBC TELEVISION'S LONG-running *Tonight Show*, invited me to be on his program while I was making my return to boxing. Johnny said, "George, they say that all the guys you are fighting are soft touches. Now tell me the truth. Is this guy you're about to fight any good?"

Nearly all boxers talk tough and brag about how they're going to kill the other guy. I said what no one was expecting:

"I hope not!" I said with a big grin and a twinkle in my eyes.

Johnny and the studio audience cracked up. I was just being honest and telling the truth, which made it even funnier, I guess. After all, what boxer wants to fight someone who will beat him up? Besides, my opponent was plenty good; he had a record of 36 wins and 3 losses; he was not exactly a pushover, especially for a boxer on the comeback trail.

I think one reason people respond so positively to my message is because I always try to be real. What you see is what you get. And that's why my commercials have been successful—because people respond to someone who genuinely believes in the product.

Many people ask, "What is the secret of success?" That's simple: Success usually comes as a result of doing things that are right and avoiding things that bring failure. Of course, God can make anyone successful, but He generally has conditions for extending His favor. He usually doesn't reward people for being lazy. Some people fail because they have poor work habits or give up too soon.

I believe success comes as a by-product of several factors. But it all begins by acknowledging God as number one on your priority list.

PUT GOD FIRST

An old adage says, "If something is worth doing, it is worth doing right." I take that one step further: You shouldn't do anything unless you do it right. And the best way to do something right is to have the proper priorities and motivation in your heart. Jesus said, "But seek first the kingdom of God and His righteousness, and all these things shall be added to you."[1] When you let God rule your life, He will provide everything else that you need.

If you'll get the top button fastened in the correct buttonhole, all the others fall into place. But if you don't get the top one right, all the other buttons on your shirt will be out of line. When God becomes your top priority, you'll be amazed at how the other areas of your life will straighten out.

> MY MISSION IS TO SERVE GOD, BUT MY "ATTACHMENTS" ARE THE SPECIFIC ASSIGNMENTS THAT HE WANTS ME TO DO.

My greatest ambition is to please the Lord. That's why I attend church services, to learn more about God and to worship Him with fellow believers. That's why I pray. That's why I live right. The Bible says, "Blessed is the man who walks not in the counsel of the ungodly . . . in His law he meditates day and night." It goes on to say, "Whatever he does shall prosper."[2] If I live to please God, He will make my life successful. Success in my book means to fulfill God's calling on my life.

The Lord has given me some tasks that I need to accomplish during my time on Earth. I call those assignments "attachments" because they're so firmly connected to my heart. My overall mission is to serve God, but my attachments are the specific assignments, the ideas He wants me to develop, the projects He wants me to pursue. In short, they make up the things on my priority list, after God. When He calls me to do something, He puts that idea in my heart and mind and then gives me the strength to do it.

For instance, I'm the minister of the Church of the Lord Jesus Christ in Houston. That's one attachment. Boxing was another attachment, but I didn't forsake being pastor so I could box. Even when I returned to the ring at age 37, I didn't neglect my pastoral responsibilities. I wasn't going to sacrifice my church to become the heavyweight champion of the world. Nothing could stop me from preaching, counseling, performing weddings and funerals, and being a friend to the members of our congregation. Sure, my boxing career took up a large amount of my time and sometimes took me away from the church when I really wanted to be there, but I found a way to fulfill both callings.

Every day, I continued going to my church office to take care of my obligations. By adding boxing to my list of attachments, I had to set my alarm to go off two hours earlier so I could run. When I boxed out of town on Saturdays, I caught a plane after the fight so I could preach the next day. After I preached in the Sunday morning service, I had a few hours to train before I spoke again in the evening service. That's when I would squeeze in fifteen rounds of boxing in the gym. I followed this rigorous schedule from 1987 to 1997. I spent ten long years working to achieve a goal that most people thought was impossible. But nothing is impossible if God is in your corner and you are willing to work hard.

Too many people want to get the prize without having to sacrifice anything. It just doesn't happen that way. You can't be a great athlete without hard work and training. You can't attain a lofty and worthy goal without significant effort. Similarly, you can't be a disciple without exercising discipline.

Even though my entire life is wrapped up in serving God, I'm not called to do everything. I can only have so many attachments in my life. My youth center and my counseling of young people is another attachment. The work I do to support colleges is another. No matter what duty I'm fulfilling at the time, I am determined to do it with excellence.

But my life is more than the goals I'm trying to achieve. No matter how significant an assignment may be, it can never become more important than God. If it ever does, the task turns into an idol. The way to prevent idolatry is to love the Lord with all your heart. That keeps the top button in the highest position, so no other button can take its place.

INCREASE YOUR MOTIVATION

Although God can use people to do great things, not everyone reaches their maximum potential. Why? I'm convinced they don't want it badly enough. Excellence isn't achieved without inspiration and perspiration. You've got to have both. Some people do just enough to get by, while others are driven to reach their goals. I call this the "bigger bass principle."

> **I ENVISIONED MYSELF WINNING THE HEAVYWEIGHT TITLE FOR TEN YEARS BEFORE I ACTUALLY CAPTURED IT.**

When I've gone fishing in east Texas, I've caught different-sized bass—some big, some small. When they stock the pond, the fish are all six or seven inches long. But if you'll go back two years later, some will be larger than others. Most will be ten inches, but a few will be huge. If they all started at the same size, why would some be larger than others?

It's because the larger ones have a bigger appetite. When they eat more, they increase in size. All fish eat enough food to survive, but the biggest ones have an insatiable hunger for more.

If you want to separate yourself from the average person, you need to develop a better appetite, to have a hunger to succeed that's beyond normal, almost an obsession. There are degrees of motivation; to me, "obsession" is motivation to the highest degree.

When your priorities are in the correct order, your greatest obsession will be to please God. Nothing works if you don't have that right. Unless you are building your life on what God wants, you shouldn't even use the word "obsession."

I've nicknamed my son George III "Monk." During Monk's first year in college, he wasn't reaching his full potential. Although he was a good student, I believed he could do better, and he needed something to motivate him. As an incentive to study harder, I made him an offer.

"Son, I have a special edition BMW X5 sport activity vehicle in my garage. If you'll get straight A's this semester, you can have it."

Monk jumped out of his chair. "What? I can have that car if I get straight A's?"

"That's what I said—but you have to get all A's. Not one B."

Immediately, Monk started hitting the books harder, studying with renewed passion. He finished the semester with an A in every course. After receiving his grades, I handed him the keys to the BMW. As he drove it around with his friends, he bragged about how hard he had to study to earn it.

Why did his grades improve? His motivation turned into an obsession, and he received a reward for his outstanding effort.

You have to keep your goal in mind and never lose sight of it. I envisioned myself winning the heavyweight title for ten years before I actually captured it. If you're not driven to do your best, you'll never reach the next level of excellence in your life. This principle can be applied to any area of your life—intellectual, physical, emotional, and spiritual. If you are obsessed with doing your best, you will succeed.

When I'm working with younger boxers in the gym, they'll work hard as long as I'm standing there watching. But if I walk away for a bit, they'll hit the punching bags for a little while—and then stop and talk. I've told those young guys they can't stop and talk when they're in an actual boxing match. They've got to fight the entire time. Those extra minutes will determine who wins when the real battle begins.

OBSESSION IS MOTIVATION TO THE HIGHEST DEGREE.

But some of those guys are just looking for an easy way to get through their workout. They like to tell their friends, "I'm a boxer." That may be true, but they'll never be able to say, "I'm a boxing champion." They aren't motivated enough to reach that level of excellence.

When I've walked into a gym where guys are lifting heavy weights, I've noticed that none of them have a book open, quietly studying how to lift weights. Instead, I hear weights clanging and lifters yelling, "ARRRRR!" as they strain every muscle, trying to push up those weights. They're so loud, it sounds like someone in the gym is trying to kill them! Their faces become contorted, and blood vessels pop out as they try to break their own personal records in weight lifting. They give it all they've got.

That's what I'm talking about. Obsession. Reading about obsession, talking about obsession, thinking about obsession—all of those things are helpful, but they are not the same as *being obsessed* by your dream to the point that you do something about it. You must experience what that obsession looks like, feels like, sounds like, and you can't fully comprehend something like that by doing it vicariously. You must experience it for yourself if your dream of success is going to come true.

RELEASE EXCESS BAGGAGE

If you want to be obsessed to be your best, you must also get rid of the negative things that are weighing you down. Are you carrying any baggage that you don't really need to be hauling around? That extra weight will slow you down and wear you out, which will keep you from being successful. You've got to let it go. The excess baggage that's killing you might be a bad habit that needs to be broken.

> JUST IMAGINE A BIG, FAT GUY, GASPING FOR AIR, BARELY ABLE TO JOG AROUND THE BLOCK, WHO CLAIMS THAT HE WILL BE THE HEAVYWEIGHT CHAMPION OF THE WORLD AGAIN!

Giving up smoking was one of the hardest things I had to do when I first began boxing. I started smoking as a kid when I stole some cigarettes from my parents. I got addicted to them and didn't think I could ever break the habit. When I had to choose between buying a pack of cigarettes or a sandwich, I'd choose the smokes.

I tried many times to quit. I'd tell myself, *I'm through,* and then be smoking again an hour later. I'd throw my cigarettes out the window, and then when no one was looking, I'd go outside and get them. If they were wet, I'd let the pack dry out and then light 'em up.

You know you're addicted when you'll smoke a stranger's tossed-away cigarette. I dug through ashtrays in office buildings, looking for half-smoked butts. If I found one, I'd slip it into my pocket and then ask someone for a light. This went on for years, until I finally decided to quit once and for all.

Drinking was also a bad problem for me. On my nineteenth birthday, I got so drunk that I couldn't remember what happened that night. The next day, I ran into my friend who had been badly beaten up. He had a swollen eye and other bruises. I asked what happened.

"Don't you remember?" he asked. "You beat me up last night!"

That stunned me. It shook me so much that I decided never to take another drink of alcohol. And I never have since then. I wouldn't be where I am today if I hadn't quit smoking and drinking.

Part of the baggage I needed to lose literally *was* weight. When I started my comeback, I had to get rid of some excess George. I was extremely over-weight. In the nearly ten years I had been out of boxing, I had ballooned from 220 to 315 pounds. And it wasn't muscle that I gained!

To shed the blubber, my menu had to be slashed. I was accustomed to eating anything that fell under the category of "food." If it was on my plate and didn't move, I stuck a fork in it. But when I became obsessed with becoming a champion again, I forced myself to quit eating sausages. I had been devouring as many as I wanted. Not anymore. I also stopped eating ice cream, cake, and cookies. To get back into an exercise regimen, I started with the basics—running every day. I was so out of shape that I couldn't go far. At first, I couldn't even make it around my block, which was about a mile. I had to stop a few times to catch my breath, huffing and puffing.

Just imagine a big, fat guy, gasping for air, barely able to jog around the block, who claims that he will be the heavyweight champion of the world again! I looked ridiculous to everyone who saw me. I'm sure they laughed as they peeked through their curtains early in the morning while I slowly shuffled past their houses. Only two people on this entire planet believed I could recapture the title—my wife and me.

But I had to get my weight down. I would walk and run, walk and run. Finally, I was able to run the whole time without walking. Then I began running longer distances, and with the combination of a proper diet and regular exercise, the fat continued to melt away. I kept running for the next eight months, until I finally got down to my fighting weight—229 pounds. The flab was fun to put on but hard to take off. However, I wouldn't have won the championship title if I first hadn't gotten rid of that extra weight.

Maybe your "extra weight" has been caused not by taking in too many calories, but by taking on an unhealthy way of life. Do you find yourself being critical of others? That's excess baggage. You'll never move up when you're cutting others down. Is a pessimistic attitude weighing you down? You won't reach success unless you believe the best will happen. Are you involved in an ungodly relationship? Whether you realize it or not, you're carrying that person around on your back.

An important step to success is to get rid of any unnecessary baggage that's hindering you from reaching your destination. Some bags are just too heavy to carry with you on the journey. Others just aren't worth the price if you truly want to be a champion.

LEARN FROM WISE PEOPLE

In the Old Testament, the prophet Elisha followed the prophet Elijah from town to town, watching and learning from him. Elijah asked him, "What do you want from me?"

"I want a double portion of your power," Elisha answered.

Elijah told him, "If you watch me go, you'll get it."

When Elijah took off in his chariot, Elisha received Elijah's power. The lesson is this: *If you want it, you've got to stick with the person who has it.* Don't try to reinvent the wheel. Just learn from the guys who have already done it

well. You need a mentor, a seasoned coach who is willing to share his wisdom and experience with you. Ask someone who has already been successful to guide you. If you'll listen to

YOU HAVE TO BE WISE ENOUGH TO LISTEN TO WISE PEOPLE.

the expert's advice, it will streamline your path and flatten out your learning curve so you won't waste time and energy.

When I was working with all those younger fighters, I'd ask, "Do you want to be a champion? Do you really want it? If you do, I'll show you how to get it."

Then they'd disappear. So many times I've tried to help boxers achieve success by taking them through the hard training. But after a couple of months, they would quit coming into the gym.

Later, I would see them training with someone else. They didn't want a former professional champion showing them what to do. It was just too grueling. They preferred to learn from a different instructor because it was easier training for them.

When I was younger, I learned a lot about boxing from a former heavyweight champion, Sonny Liston. He taught me about the intensity of training that would be required to win the title. I also received instruction from another great heavyweight champion, Joe Louis.

I told Joe that I got tired when I fought. He asked, "How far do you run?"

"Three miles a day."

Louis said, "Run six."

Joe knew that I wasn't training hard enough. If I wanted to win the title, I needed to double my efforts. People tend to want that secret little formula for success without having to do the hard work. But hard work *is* the secret little formula.

When I started seriously training for the heavyweight title the second time, I hired Angelo Dundee as my trainer because he was the best in the business. I listened to his advice because he knew how to win championships. If you want to be a champion in your field, you must be willing to listen to wise people who have been where you

> YOU NEED A MENTOR, A SEASONED COACH WHO IS WILLING TO SHARE HIS WISDOM AND EXPERIENCE WITH YOU.

want to go, or at least can point you in the right direction. Learning from an expert will channel your hard work into the right areas so you won't waste your time and energy doing things that are unnecessary.

DON'T GIVE UP

Discouragement is your greatest enemy when you're in the middle of a difficult battle. You have to be determined to make it to the end. You cannot give up. The willpower inside your heart weakens every time you throw in the towel. Once you quit the first time, it's ten times easier to quit the second time. You have to tell yourself, *I'm going to keep going until I cross the finish line. I'm not going to give up. I will not quit.*

When I first started boxing, I often went running with other fighters. After a while, they would drop out and I would be the only one still running. The loneliest journey is the road to the heavyweight championship of the world. Nobody wants to run those extra miles with you.

Remember, when I retired from boxing after the Jimmy Young fight, I stopped training for almost ten years. After I decided to return to the sport, getting my body back into shape was much harder than the first time. When I was younger, I didn't have to lose any weight. But now it seemed like it took me forever to get down to 300 pounds.

One day, after I'd been training for a while, I made up my mind that I was going to run ten miles, which was much farther than I had been jogging. To make sure I wouldn't quit before I reached my goal, I asked my wife to meet me at a certain place ten miles away to pick me up.

ONCE YOU QUIT THE FIRST TIME, IT'S TEN TIMES EASIER TO QUIT THE SECOND TIME.

After running just three miles, I had to fight off thoughts that attacked my mind: *I'm ready to quit. I'm not going to make it. I might as well stop.* I had to win the battle inside my mind if my legs were going to keep moving. Kicking those thoughts out of my mind, I pressed on toward the fourth mile. Now I was cheering myself on. *Keep going, George. You're racing toward the championship.* Five miles. I kept trotting, one mile at a time, and before I knew it, I saw my wife waiting for me.

After a while, I was running ten, fifteen, and even seventeen miles at times, getting ready for my big chance at the title. But everywhere I went, people were telling me that I was too old to be boxing. I could easily have allowed their words to discourage me, although that was probably not their intent. But I shook off those negative comments and kept running.

One day I was running down the street when a neighbor about my age yelled to me, "Hey, George, ease up. We need to be careful about running at our age." Telling me to quit wasn't what I needed to hear when I was already tired!

I thought, *This guy just doesn't understand how much he can do at his age. He could be running with me if he wanted.* He walked back into his house, but I just kept going and finished my seventeen-mile workout.

After I won the championship at age forty-five, he congratulated me and said, "We can do anything!"

"Yes, sir," I said with a smile. "*We* can."

Don't listen to those who try to discourage you from fulfilling God's call. You've got a job to do, and the One you'll have to answer to is the One who created you. If He is pleased with how you've run your race, you've been a success.

TIPS FROM GEORGE'S CORNER
ON FINDING SUCCESS

- Put God first and seek to please Jesus in everything you do.
- Increase your motivation to the highest degree.
- Eliminate whatever is slowing you down.
- Find a godly mentor and follow his advice.
- Don't give in to thoughts of quitting.

15

DO YOUR GIVING WHILE YOU'RE LIVING

MANY PEOPLE FIND IT EASY TO RECEIVE MONEY BUT SO MUCH harder to give it away. Someone once said that you can't go through life wearing two catcher's mitts. You need to throw something back!

If you're only receiving and never giving, you'll end up spiritually stagnate and life will be boring. If that describes how you feel, and you want to be rejuvenated, reverse the process and start giving. Take some of the things that you have received and give them away.

Some people do all their giving in one big lump sum—after they die. When they write their wills, they bequeath all their earthly possessions to family and charitable organizations. Passing down an inheritance is a part of good stewardship and can help fund institutions and future generations.

While it's good to leave an inheritance, it's even better to do some of your giving while you're living. If you wait until you're dead to disperse your money, you'll never experience the thrill of helping someone. I learned how to give when I revisited the neighborhood where I grew up.

MY FIRST LESSON IN GIVING

Before I knew Jesus, I bought whatever I wanted and never thought much about helping others. I loved to show off my new cars, trying to impress everyone. That's what I lived for. I was consumed with getting, not giving.

But after having my encounter with God, my attitude changed. Instead of accumulating more for myself, I wanted to start sharing with others. I recalled my childhood friends I grew up with when my family was poor and had next to nothing as far as material things. When I became famous, I conveniently forgot about my old friends because my new friends were all celebrities. Now that I knew the Ultimate Giver, I decided to go back to my old neighborhood and give out some gifts.

> YOU CAN'T GO THROUGH LIFE WEARING TWO CATCHER'S MITTS. YOU NEED TO THROW SOMETHING BACK.

I saw my cousin, James Carpenter, walking down the street, so I pulled over and gave him a ride. He had been incarcerated for a number of years and was trying to start life over.

"James, it's good to see you again," I said. "What have you been up to since you've been out?"

"Well, George, I've applied for a job on Buffalo Speedway, and I think I'm going to get it."

I was glad to see he was making an effort to find work. "That's great, James. How are you getting around without a car?"

He said, "I can catch the bus, and then transfer to another bus. . . ."

Immediately I thought about a new car that I had at my training camp in Marshall, Texas. "James, how would you like a car of your own? It won't cost you a penny."

"My own car?" he said excitedly. "You'll give me a car? That is exactly what I need!"

He had been hoping for some kind of a break in life. Now he could get to his job without having to catch buses. James received a new start in life, thanks to that vehicle.

The thrill of giving him that car and seeing his reaction—along with the satisfaction of knowing how much it helped him—was one of the greatest feelings that I've ever experienced. I began to understand what Jesus meant when He said, "It is more blessed to give than to receive."[1] The joy of giving away that car far exceeded the happiness I felt when I bought it.

That was such a good experience for me that I started giving away other cars to people in need. The thrill almost became addictive. I wanted to assist everyone who truly needed help.

That's how I began giving. Maybe you're wondering how you can get started. Many organizations are already helping people but desperately need funds to keep the work going. You can be a tremendous help by giving your money to those ministries.

HELPING GOOD CAUSES

One way that you can give to the Lord is by helping to support God's house, your local place of worship. When you do that, be sure to say a silent prayer as you give: *Lord, I'm giving this offering because I love You and want to help expand Your kingdom.* Do all you can to support those organizations that will use your gift to preach and teach God's Word so more people will come to know Jesus or know Him better.

Whenever you give a donation, don't draw attention to yourself or your gift. That's not the right motive. Do your giving privately so that only the Lord sees what you're doing. That doesn't mean that it's wrong if someone finds out. I'm informing you about my giving not to draw attention to myself, but to inspire you to help others. The more people who discover how enjoyable and rewarding it is to give, the better off this world will be.

Some people like to give to ministries and mission organizations, which are all good causes. Others enjoy giving to colleges of their choice. I like to help colleges around the nation by setting up scholarship funds. Because God has a plan for everyone, I believe strongly in education, in getting prepared for what the good Lord wants to do in and through a person's life.

Sometimes students need assistance to get to that next educational level so they can fulfill their calling.

You can help those who are less fortunate in tangible ways. If your parents are struggling financially, you need to support them so they don't have to worry about their electricity being cut off. They supplied your needs as you grew up, so now you need to return the favor. Sometimes people will give their last dime to the church but won't take care of their own families.

DON'T GIVE YOUR MONEY TO DRAW ATTENTION TO YOURSELF.

Jesus got angry at the religious group called the Pharisees because they were forbidding people from helping their needy parents. They created a tradition that violated God's commandment to honor your father and mother.

According to the Pharisees, any person could withhold support from a needy parent simply by declaring that the money was vowed to the temple as a sacred gift. Instead of using their money to help their parents, they handed it over to a priest. The Pharisees made up this tradition because they were greedy and wanted the money for themselves instead of using it to help the poor.

Whether you're giving to your church, a college, a needy parent, or some other worthy cause, make sure that you do it with a cheerful heart and not grudgingly. You don't want to miss the thrill of giving.

AN ACT OF WORSHIP

Whether you realize it or not, giving is one of the ways that you can worship God. Have you read the story in the Bible about the guy who went to the altar and presented his offering of *nothing* to God? You've never read that because it's not in there. The worshipers always presented *something* to God—their money, an animal, or produce from their harvest. You will always give to that which you love the most. It's your act of worship.

You may be thinking, *George, I'm too poor to give.* God certainly understands your financial situation, but everyone can contribute something. No matter how poor you may be, you can still be a giver. You can give your time to a worthy cause; you can give a helping hand or a gift of love to somebody who desperately needs it. Oddly enough, giving is the way out of your poverty. The more you give to help others, the more God gives back to you.

One time Jesus pointed out to His disciples a poor widow who gave her last two coins in the temple treasury box. He didn't scold her for being foolish but praised her for being generous. He explained that in God's eyes, her small gift was actually more than all the other contributors combined.

Why was her gift greater? Because after making her contribution, she had nothing left to live on. She had to trust God to meet her needs. Do you think the Lord let her starve to death? No way! The widow's offering shows that no one is too poor to give.

Don't offer God your leftovers after you've bought what you want. Put Him first in your life. Give Him the best offering that you're able to afford. And do it cheerfully. In Genesis, Cain and Abel both made offerings to the Lord. The Lord accepted Abel's offering but rejected Cain's because he gave it with a bad attitude. God doesn't just look at the amount, but also looks at your attitude when you give it.

> **YOU WILL ALWAYS GIVE TO THAT WHICH YOU LOVE THE MOST.**

The Lord promises that when you give, He will open the windows of heaven to pour out for you a blessing so large that you can't even contain it. It takes faith to let go of something you have, which makes you poorer at first. But that's not the end of the story. When God opens those windows in heaven, He will more than make up for whatever you gave on Earth.

HELPING THE POOR

I'll never forget what it was like to grow up in abject poverty. It didn't just affect my stomach; it influenced my whole being. Poverty produces a feeling of hopelessness. I didn't think that life would ever get better. It was so hard to get the things we needed to live. I spent much of my time walking up and down the street looking for money, hoping to find a lost wallet. Eventually I started mugging people to get cash and didn't even feel bad about it. Many poor kids will steal simply because it's the only way they know how to survive.

Being poverty-stricken affected the way I interpreted life. I remember watching a television show when I was boy, but the only thing I saw was the food they were eating! It wasn't until after I grew up that I realized that *Leave It to Beaver* was a comedy. I was amazed that Wally and Beaver each had their own bed. They even had their own bathroom and bathtub. It was hard for me to comprehend such wealth.

Getting out of the slums was no easy task. Getting the slums out of me was even tougher. Poor people feel hopeless. It almost takes a miracle to pull a person out of poverty. The sociological wall that divides the rich and poor has to come down. The wealthy class often looks down on the poor as "those people." And deprived people view the rich as cold and heartless. The way to break down the barrier between the rich and poor is to associate with each other and to help one another. Make a connection. If you can break down that barrier, it may pave the way to recovery for some person, a family, maybe an entire community.

I still remember one of my first encounters with a "rich" person. When I was a boy, a woman asked me to cut her grass. She probably wasn't wealthy, but she seemed rich to me because she had a yard. After I mowed the grass, she gave me a sandwich, talked with me, and treated me with tremendous kindness. She made me feel really good, like I was important and my life mattered. At that moment, she wasn't a rich person talking to a poor person. We were just two people talking. She broke down the barrier.

Now that I have escaped from poverty, I won't forget those who are less fortunate. I have a burning desire to reach troubled youth. I used to go out and preach on the streets because I wanted those kids to find God. They would listen to me on the sidewalk but would never show up at church. When that didn't work like I had hoped, I prayed to find a better way to reach them.

That's when the Lord gave me the idea to start a youth center. In that way, I could help kids who would never step inside a church. I wouldn't preach to them but would just be available if they ever needed to talk. My plan was to befriend them and hopefully become a role model they would follow.

Although the youth center was a great idea, it didn't pop into existence like a wish fulfilled by a genie. It took a lot of money to make it happen. I had set aside some money that I had planned to use for my retirement. After praying about it, I knew that account could be used to build the center. I wanted to invest my money to change lives. That was my gift to the Lord during a crucial time in my life.

The George Foreman Youth Center was constructed in 1983 and is still reaching young people today. I've spent a lot of my time at the center with kids, trying to influence them in a positive way. My life is devoted to doing more of that in the future.

GOD ALWAYS REWARDS

Even when I was broke, I kept preaching about God's faithfulness to provide for me. King David said, "I have been young, and now am old; yet I have not seen the righteous forsaken, his descendants begging bread."[2] Over his entire lifetime, David had *never* seen God's servants out begging for bread. It was true for me, too. After I trusted God, I always had something to eat. The Lord always came through, even when times were tough.

And my desperate financial situation never stopped me from giving. I remembered Jesus' promise: "Give, and it will be given to you; good measure, pressed down, shaken together, running over, they will pour into your lap. For by your standard of measure it will be measured to you in return."[3]

Jesus used this description to show how God will generously reward those who give. He won't just give a good measure but will keep pouring out the blessings until they overflow onto the person who gave the gift. The contributor will receive back far more than he ever gave, and the reward will extend into eternity.

Although the Lord has promised to reward those who give, you won't find me saying, "I've done this for God, so now He is going to do something for me." My motive for giving isn't to get something back from God. However, the Lord has seen what I've done and has rewarded me for my giving. It's almost like He says, "Because you did this for Me, I want to bless you in return."

WHEN YOU GIVE YOUR MONEY ON EARTH, IT'S BEING DEPOSITED IN HEAVEN.

God will reward your generosity not only in the here and now, but also in eternity. Every Christian has an "IRA" (Individual Rewards Account) in heaven. Jesus said, "Lay up *for yourselves* treasures in heaven."[4] You have your own personal account in the next world. The way you make deposits in your heavenly account is by cheerfully helping others during your time on Earth. When you give your money here, it's being deposited up there. The only time you can send up treasure is while you're alive. After you die, you can't make any more deposits.

Although you can't see the transactions take place between Earth and heaven, you'll see them when you get to heaven. Your treasure will be waiting for you. And then, as you worship God, you'll be able to enjoy your reward throughout all eternity.

So it really doesn't matter if I get repaid here on Earth for my giving. I'm looking forward to being rewarded in heaven, which is wealth that will last forever.

TIPS FROM GEORGE'S CORNER
ON GIVING

- Always give cheerfully, not grudgingly.
- Find a way to help those who are less fortunate.
- Give your best to God, not your leftovers.
- Remember that the Lord will reward you far beyond your gift.

16
AGE FORTY ISN'T A DEATH SENTENCE

ON MY THIRTY-SEVENTH BIRTHDAY, I BROKE DOWN AND CRIED. I thought life was over, and I hadn't even reached forty yet. After I pulled myself out of the doldrums, I decided to return to boxing. Everyone said, "George is too old to box. Those young guys will kill him!"

When I turned forty, boxing experts thought it was time for me to hang up the gloves. The great trainer Gil Clancy said, "Boxing has too many retreads. What is George Foreman doing out there boxing? He shouldn't be fighting."

As the calendar pages turned, I wasn't getting any younger and the skeptics weren't getting any kinder. What was an old man like me doing in the boxing ring, fighting guys half my age and in much better physical condition? In spite of what the critics said, I was winning every match.

They said I was too old at forty-one. Really old at forty-two. Should be on a respirator at forty-three. Age forty-four? Nearly in the grave. Age forty-five, heavyweight champion of the world! I am the oldest person to ever capture the title.

I did what everyone said was impossible—but only because God was in my corner. He said, "Let Me show you what I can do through you." Sure, I worked hard, trained hard, and had to fight my way from the bottom to the top. But each step of the way, God gave me the ability to do it. And He still has more things for me to accomplish before I'm done on Earth.

> **GOD WAS WAITING FOR MOSES TO TURN EIGHTY YEARS OLD SO HE COULD GIVE HIM A FRESH ASSIGNMENT.**

I sometimes tell people that I want to live until I'm one hundred forty-four years old so I can keep testifying about the good Lord. I have so much more I want to accomplish that it may take that long to get it all done. I don't want to even entertain the idea of dying until I've finished everything God has called me to do.

As I grow older, I want the optometrist to keep prescribing me stronger glasses until my eyes don't work anymore. Only then will I quit trying to see. I want to use up every bit of strength, even down to wiggling every finger and toe. Before they put me in the casket, let me wear out my wheelchair and walker. And then, when I've finally used up everything God has given me, I'll consider life over.

YOU'RE JUST GETTING STARTED

Do you think life is over because you've turned forty, fifty, or even sixty years of age? No way. You're just getting started! Moses was an old man when God spoke to him through a burning bush that was not consumed. When Moses fled from Egypt to the land of Midian, he planned to retire there. But God was just waiting for Moses to turn eighty years old so He could give him a fresh assignment. The Lord said, "Moses, I have a job for you to do. I want you to lead the Hebrew nation out of Egyptian bondage. But you won't be able to do it in your own strength. You'll have to depend on My strength."

Moses received his calling from God at the right time in his life. His story is a reminder for every generation that the Lord isn't finished with you simply because you have reached a certain age. As long as you're alive, God still has a plan for your life. If you'll keep progressing and learning as you grow older, you can be more effective at sixty years of age than when you were at twenty.

Many people in the Bible received their divine assignments when they were considered ready for the rest home. Caleb was eighty-five years old when he captured the city of Hebron. Sarah gave birth to Isaac at age ninety, and Abraham became a dad at one hundred years old. That just goes to show us that age doesn't matter when God wants to accomplish something.

He can do the same with you and me. As long as we believe that God can work through us, all things are possible. With God in your corner, you can do anything—no matter what your age. You're only limited by your own unbelief.

STARTING AT THE BOTTOM

When I made my boxing comeback, I decided I was going to start over at the bottom. I had researched all those fighters who had come out of retirement because I wanted to discover why they didn't succeed. They were all great boxers, but they failed to ascend to the top again following their retirement. I concluded that they had all taken the wrong approach.

When former heavyweight champ Joe Louis tried to make his comeback from retirement, he was immediately offered a shot at the title. Rocky Marciano almost killed Louis in that fight. Louis tried to get back to the top too quickly and wasn't ready. Former heavyweight champion Joe Frazier also came out of retirement to fight again. He trained for about a week and looked horrible in a losing effort.

I WANT TO LIVE UNTIL I'M 144 YEARS OLD.

Every boxer coming out of retirement to fight again had one thing in common—they were on top when they left and thought they could start over at the top. That was their mistake; they tried to return to the top too quickly. They assumed they didn't have enough time to start over at the bottom.

My boxing advisers told me, "You'd better hurry up because time is running out for you." They wanted me to follow the same failed strategy as my retired predecessors—start over at the top while I still had some ability left. But I wasn't going to follow the others and fail. Instead, I was going to do the opposite.

Everyone thought I was crazy when I told them my plan. "I'm not going to try to get a title shot for several years. I'll start over at the bottom and slowly work my way back to the top."

My friends looked at me like I had lost my mind, but I knew it would take at least three years to get my timing back. There was no other way around it.

I spent hundreds of hours watching boxing film and reading articles, trying to learn how I could improve my timing. I studied all the great boxers and researched old sports clippings. I read everything I could find about track, boxing, and even football in the 1930s through the 1950s. Perhaps they used techniques that we've forgotten about today. My extensive research helped me become a smarter boxer than I was previously.

USING AGE AS AN ADVANTAGE

I don't view myself as getting older, but as graduating to a higher level in life. I've gained insights from every year that I've lived. My experiences have added greater depth and value to my life, which has taught me to make better transitions as I've grown older. Instead of relying on abilities that become weaker over time, I've capitalized on those skills that become stronger with age.

> I DON'T VIEW MYSELF AS GETTING OLDER, BUT AS GRADUATING TO A HIGHER LEVEL IN LIFE.

When I was a young boxer, my greatest asset was my speed. The great boxer Sugar Ray Robinson told me, "It doesn't matter how you throw your punches as long as you can do it quickly." But after being retired from boxing for ten years, my speed and instincts had deteriorated.

As I studied the boxers who had tried to come back from retirement, I noticed they were using the same techniques as when they were younger. But they couldn't function at their previous performance level, and their opponents quickly sent them back into retirement.

Instead of following in their footsteps, I decided to try something new. If I was going to be champ again, I would have to find a way to compensate for my lack of speed. It forced me to learn a new way to box. Even though I had the desire inside me to win the title, my physical skills didn't measure up. My new style of boxing had to be completely different than the way I had moved around in the ring before. I had to find another method for defending myself, too, like changing the position of my hands for better protection.

> EVERY BOXER COMING OUT OF RETIREMENT TO FIGHT AGAIN HAD ONE THING IN COMMON—THEY WERE ON TOP WHEN THEY LEFT AND THOUGHT THEY COULD START OVER AT THE TOP.

I couldn't run fast anymore, but I could walk. Walking strengthened the muscles I needed for endurance. No longer would I depend on the quick knockout, but I would work on improving my stamina so I could stay in the ring for the full twelve rounds. That may sound like an easy task, but I had to spar with the young guys in the gym, and making all those adjustments wasn't easy at first.

After doing some soul-searching, I knew that I couldn't recapture the heavyweight title unless I first won the fight going on inside my mind. I had to believe I could win it before I could actually do it. So instead of being frustrated about learning a new way to box, I decided to prove to the world that no one is too old to start over.

With a renewed outlook, I realized my age could be used to my advantage instead of being a disadvantage. All of my past experience gave me an edge over the younger boxers. When I first started boxing as a young man, I didn't know how to do anything. I couldn't skip rope. I couldn't hit the speed bags. Everything that I needed to learn seemed impossible at that time. Yet by the time I was twenty-four years old, I was considered the best at skipping rope, hitting the speed bags, and running in preparation for a boxing match.

Learning a new way to box wouldn't be as difficult as beginning from scratch. If I could start from the bottom and win the championship, surely I could take my abilities to another level if I used a new technique and found a better way to utilize my skills.

And that's what I've found with age: if you've already done something once, you can do it again. If you've started at the bottom and learned a particular skill, your experience puts you ahead of the game.

When I was young, I succeeded by using my stamina, muscles, and energy. But as time passed, my former strengths turned into weaknesses. As I've grown older, I've gained insights about life through my experiences, which has more than compensated for my loss of vigor. My age has actually become my asset. Know-how has become more valuable than raw ability.

If you have turned forty, you have so much more practical knowledge than younger people, simply because of the lessons you've learned. If God already gave you certain abilities when you were younger, He can refine them if you need to start over.

LEARNING TO BOX WITHOUT HATE

I had been retired for ten years and hadn't trained at all during that time. But after all of my investments had gone under, I needed to do something to provide for my family and pay the mortgage on the George Foreman Youth and Community Center. After praying about it, I decided to return to the sport.

But I had an advantage my second time around that I didn't have the first time—faith in God. As I've mentioned in previous chapters, King David's sentiment inspired me to look up to the good Lord. King David said, "I've *never* seen the righteous for-

I HAD TO LEARN A NEW WAY TO BOX—WITHOUT HATE.

saken." Even though no one else believed I could become champion, I still believed. I knew that if I continued to work hard, God would bless my efforts.

I had walked away from boxing after my dramatic post-fight conversion experience because the only way I had known how to fight was in anger. When I boxed as a younger man, I balled my fist as tight as I could when I hit my opponents because I wanted to hurt them. I viewed them as animals to be hunted. My opponents weren't human beings—they were the enemy. As I stood in the ring and looked at the other fighter, I'd say to myself, *I'm going to kill him.*

When I decided to get back into the sport, I had to learn a new way to box—without hate. Many of the kids who came into my youth center wanted to be boxers. I taught them, "Never throw a punch in anger. This is an honorable sport; it's been around for thousands of years. You don't need a killer instinct to win a match."

One of my favorite verses is, "Blessed are the meek, for they shall inherit the earth."[1] Not that they will *conquer* the earth, but they will *inherit* it. You don't have to destroy someone to get what you want. Do it God's way, and you'll inherit it.

So in my comeback, I never threw one punch in anger. Instead of tightening my fist into a ball, I never closed up my hand. I knew I couldn't seriously hurt anyone if my fist wasn't tight. In boxing, like any sport, you can control what you do. I never injured anyone inside the ring in any of my matches during my second career in boxing.

Sometimes I got booed during my comeback because I wouldn't destroy my opponents like I had done before. In my fight against Dwight Muhammad Qawi in Las Vegas, I heard some spectators yell, "Get tough, George!" I found out later they wanted a fast knockout because they had bet on the rounds.

Before I fought Evander Holyfield, I had a dream that I killed him in the ring. When I fought him a few days later for the championship, I stunned him with a punch and he held on to me. If I were the old George, I would have finished him off right then. But as soon as he held on to me, the dream popped in my mind. I was afraid that if I hit him again at that point, I might truly regret it. So I let him hold on and clear his head. I ended up losing the championship bout, but I would have rather lost the fight than seen that awful dream come true.

Being older, I had to fight smarter. Instead of relying on my power, I had to concentrate on finding the weaknesses in my opponents, which I usually did. Similarly, I lost a lot of speed and quickness, which forced me to train differently so I could gain endurance. That is why on most days, I ran ten, fifteen, or seventeen miles.

When I boxed in my younger years, I usually knocked out the guys early so I didn't need to fight in the later rounds. But this time, I learned to use my wisdom more than my power. I wasn't going to stand toe-to-toe and get my head beat in. Instead, I learned how to deflect punches so they couldn't hit me. I had run all those miles in training so I could have the energy to last the entire fight. When friends asked me why I was running so much, I told them, "I'm either going to lose my knees or lose my brains. I choose the knees."

You might say, "George, you *did* knock out your opponents during your comeback. How can you say you didn't hurt them?"

I learned how to box so I could win the bout without injuring my opponent. If you're not familiar with boxing, a "knockout" doesn't always mean to be knocked *unconscious*. In most bouts, when a boxer falls to the canvas three times in a round, it counts as a knockout. Sometimes the referee will stop a fight even when a boxer hasn't been knocked down, which counts as a knockout. He's protecting the boxer from being seriously hurt by stopping the fight before it gets to that point.

When I fought before I gave my life to God, I started building up my rage on Friday to get ready for my match on Saturday. By the time of the fight, I was ready to explode with hatred. When I met my opponent in the middle of the ring to receive the referee's instructions, I would get nose-to-nose and stare him in the eyes. I wanted him to see me fuming so he would be afraid of me.

But in my new career of boxing, I didn't do that. I was going to be the "good George" the entire time, from the beginning of my training to after I climbed into the ring. I wanted my children to see me on television as a good man—not a mean, hateful guy. I met all my opponents in the middle of the ring with a big smile on my face. Ironically, they thought I was trying to psyche them out! Sometimes I could hear their trainers yelling at them, "Don't look at him! He's trying to mess with your mind." But I was just being friendly; I wanted to let them know that boxing was a sport to me and that I wasn't angry at them.

Some people asked me, "How can you be a preacher and a boxer?"

"That's real easy," I replied. "Just come to church with me on Sunday, and then come get in the ring with me on Monday. You won't ask that question again."

The truth is, I did change my approach to boxing after I became a preacher. I developed more of a classic regard for boxing—as a sport requiring skill and strategy, not simply raw power. I didn't go into the ring with the intent to pulverize my opponent. I went into the ring to win, but not to hurt my opponent any more than necessary. I jokingly told some of my opponents, "I don't want to hurt you; I just want to knock you out!"

THE YOUNG AND THE BREATHLESS

Starting at the bottom meant that I would be fighting supposedly easier opponents at first. I was frequently matched against young, inexperienced guys or older, unknown fighters who were just trying to earn one more paycheck. Talk show hosts joked, "George, you're fighting guys on a respirator."

"That's not true!" I replied, pretending to be insulted. "They have to be off the respirator for five days before I'll fight them!"

My first professional fight after coming out of retirement in March 1987 was in Sacramento, California. I defeated a tough fighter named Steve Zouski, but the most gratifying part of the event took place before the bout even began. When I stepped into the ring, the crowd gave me a standing ovation. I had never before received such an ovation as a boxer, not even when I was the world champion. But with their enthusiastic applause, the crowd was saying, "Welcome back, George." And I appreciated it more than I knew how to express.

I earned $21,000 for my victory that night, a good amount, but a far cry from what I had been making when I retired from boxing twenty years earlier. Now, on the comeback trail, instead of making $5 million like before, I'd go from city to city, boxing for $500, $1,000, or $2,500. I didn't make any profit during my first two comeback years because I had to pay my sparring partners and others who worked for me. I was barely hanging on financially. After I paid my team, I had nothing left.

> I TOLD PEOPLE, "I'M EITHER GOING TO LOSE MY KNEES OR LOSE MY BRAINS. I CHOOSE THE KNEES."

Eventually, I started making more money—$5,000, $8,000, $12,000. By now I was primarily interested in getting promoted with sports writers and local television interviews. If I was ever going to get a shot at the championship again, I needed more publicity. I started campaigning like a politician, with the excitement of an automobile salesman.

If the local sports news program promised to give me one minute of airtime, I would try to make it the most dynamic sixty seconds on television. "George, we hear that you're going back in the ring. Is that a good idea for a man your age?"

I'd excitedly say, "Yep! They say that age forty is a death sentence, but I'm going to show you that an old guy like me can beat *anybody*, at *any time!*"

The viewers loved it. People would talk about it the next day at the office watercooler. Then the local sports news director would call me back again for a three-minute interview. Other shows would give me five or ten minutes. I made every interview as exciting as possible.

Mike Tyson, who was the champion at the time, wouldn't speak to the press. But I was willing to give interviews at any time, day or night. Reporters kept coming back to me because Tyson wouldn't talk to them.

Whenever I was in a press conference with a room full of reporters, I always joked with them and answered every one of their questions. I'd say, "I have to keep fighting because it is the only thing that keeps me out of the hamburger joints. If I don't fight, I'll eat this planet."

> **I WALKED BACK TO MY CORNER THINKING, MAYBE I SHOULDN'T HAVE RETURNED TO BOXING.**

When asked why I hadn't knocked out a particular opponent, I quipped, "My mother was watching on television, and she doesn't want me to hurt anyone." The media guys loved my quotes and put me on the front pages of their newspapers and magazines. Nike called me to do a shoe commercial because the reporters had boosted my popularity.

Because I decided to be my own manager, I strategically picked the matches I wanted to fight. I chose opponents who could prepare me for tougher boxers. That was my plan—to slowly work my way up the rankings. But I almost made a big mistake, which nearly sent me back into retirement.

NEARLY DEFEATED

For my third fight during my comeback, a promoter tried to set up a match for me. He said, "George, we've got a guy by the name of Bobby Crabtree for you to fight."

"Is he tough?" I asked.

"He's real tough, and he'll come after you. You won't have to go looking for him." I agreed to the match because that was the kind of boxer I wanted to fight. If he had been the type to run away from me or dance around the ring, it would have been hard for me to beat him.

Later, I heard a rumor that Crabtree didn't fight like the promoter had told me. Someone who had seen him box told me, "That guy's not going to come after you; he'll try to stay away. Plus, he's a southpaw." (Southpaws are left-handed boxers, who are more difficult to fight.)

I knew I'd better find out if the report was true. I asked Brent Bowers, one of my sparring partners, to go check out Bobby Crabtree. "Be sure to ask him for his autograph," I said.

Brent went and introduced himself to Bobby. He said, "I've heard a lot about you. Can I have your autograph?"

Crabtree signed the autograph with his left hand. It was true; he was a southpaw and not the type of boxer I had been led to believe. I would have prepared wrongly if I hadn't learned this, and it might have caused me to lose the match.

I almost backed out of the fight but changed my mind. Even though the promoter who set up the fight hadn't been honest with me, I decided to honor my commitment.

When the bell rang to start the fight, Crabtree began jumping and moving around the ring. He was hitting me, but I couldn't connect a punch because he was moving too much. In the third round, his manager yelled, "Now get him! His old legs are tired." Bobby started pouring it on me.

After the round, I walked back to my corner thinking, *Maybe I shouldn't have returned to boxing.* This guy was winning the fight and I was exhausted. In the next round, I moved my right foot in front of my left foot, which was the opposite way I naturally stand when I fight. It threw him off, and I was able to connect with a shot that ended the fight.

That match almost stopped me from making my comeback. Bobby Crabtree—that's a name I'll never forget. It was one of the toughest matches I fought during my second career of boxing. But that fight made me realize that I was bringing out the best in all my opponents. They all wanted to be able to say they had beaten the former heavyweight champion.

Maybe you're attempting a comeback in your life. It won't be easy at first, but don't give up at the first sign of difficulty, struggle, or opposition. Perhaps it's time to change your strategy. Making that one little adjustment with my feet made a difference between winning and losing. Who knows what success might be yours simply by making a few changes. Maybe it's not a major area that needs adjusting; perhaps it's some habit or minor lifestyle change that could totally alter your future and lead you to a whole new level of success and satisfaction.

SEVEN YEARS LATER

Over seven years had passed since I had come out of retirement. My comeback record stood at 27 wins and 2 losses, with both defeats being for the heavyweight championship of the world. I hoped to get one more shot at the title.

Michael Moorer had just defeated Evander Holyfield on the judges' scorecards to win the heavyweight title. While working as part of the fight broadcast team, I made a controversial comment that upset some people; I said that I didn't agree with the judges' decision because I thought Holyfield had won the fight.

I called my friend, Bob Arum, who was a promoter for Top Rank Boxing. "Did you hear my comments about the Holyfield fight?" I asked.

"Yeah, I heard. George, you were just telling the truth," he replied. I could almost see Bob smiling on the other end of the line. "You want another shot at that title, don't you?"

I really hadn't called him for that reason, but I wasn't going to turn down the opportunity. "Yeah, I sure would."

That night, I dreamed I was boxing Michael Moorer. The fight had gone on for a number of rounds when I threw a left hook that set up the winning punch, a quick right. In my dream, Michael Moorer went down and I had regained the title of heavyweight champion.

After waking up, I called Bob Arum again. "Yes, I definitely want that title shot."

"Okay, George," Bob replied. "I'll start working on it."

True to his word, Bob worked out a deal for me to fight Moorer for the championship title on November 5, 1994. I started preparing for the bout by practicing in the gym to throw a left hook like I had seen in my dream. If I won this fight, I would become the oldest heavyweight champion in history. I began hyping my old age in all my pre-fight interviews: "When I win the heavyweight championship, I want every forty-year-old and fifty-year-old to stand up and have a toast of Geritol for George Foreman!"

In all the fights that I had won, I had purposely avoided saying anything about God during my interviews. Reporters often asked, "How do you keep winning at your age, George?"

I'd deflect their question by replying, "Hello, Momma," and waving at the television camera. Instead of trying to sound religious, I'd make a funny comment like, "It's time to go find me a cheeseburger!" I had seen too many boxers beat up someone and then say, "I give all praise to God." It didn't seem right, so I never talked about God after winning a fight.

But before my match with Michael Moorer for the world heavyweight title, I prayed, "Lord, I've never talked about You on television after winning my fights. But if You'll allow me to win this one tonight, I'll get on my knees and say, 'Thank You, Jesus.'"

It had been twenty years since I lost my title to Muhammad Ali, and now was my last chance to get it back. My plan was to win the fight by the three-knockdown rule, which meant I would win if my opponent went down three times in one round. Less than an hour before the bout began, the referee came to my dressing room and said, "George, the three-knockdown rule will not be in effect in this fight." Since Moorer was the champion, he had the privilege of deciding how the match would be fought, and he didn't want that rule in place.

I was shocked. Apparently Michael thought he could get knocked down four or five times and still win the fight. The change in rules forced me to adjust my strategy at the last minute. The three-knockdown rule had always prevented me from injuring my opponent. Without it, the fight would keep going on, no matter how many times I knocked him down. Now I would have to hit him hard enough so that he either wouldn't want to get up or couldn't get up.

Moorer was the first left-handed heavyweight champion in the history of boxing and he proved difficult to fight. Because he had changed the rules, I knew he would probably win most of the rounds until I could knock him out.

At the opening bell, he came at me flicking quick jabs. I didn't want to knock him down too early because I knew he would stay away from me the rest of the fight. Whenever he threw a combination, I'd return it with a jab, making sure each one connected. Although he was throwing more punches, mine eventually took a toll on him; I noticed his legs weakening. He wasn't moving as quickly, and he seemed less stable.

As the fight wore on, Moorer landed a lot of shots, with a few that really hurt. Whenever he threw his left, I countered it with a hard right. Although it appeared he was winning, I knew it was just a matter of time before he would be open for a knockdown. If I could only find an opening like I had in my dream . . .

Normally between rounds, boxers will sit on the stools in their corners and rest for a minute. But when I went back to my corner, I didn't sit down on the stool to rest. Instead, I stood the entire time and listened to the advice from my corner men, Angelo Dundee and Charley Shipes. I wanted the judges as well as Michael Moorer to know that I was still strong and ready to fight. Then I would turn around and study Moorer's body posture to see how tired he appeared. I could tell that my jabs were draining him of strength with each round. If I could only find an open shot for my left hook . . .

GOD HAD ALLOWED ME TO BECOME THE OLDEST HEAVYWEIGHT BOXING CHAMPION OF ALL TIME AT THE AGE OF FORTY-FIVE.

By the eighth round, Michael was far ahead on points. It became obvious to everyone that if the fight went the distance, he would win on the judges' scorecards. But that wasn't going to happen. I threw a left hook that hit him under the right armpit, which dropped his hands and made it harder for him to defend himself. Every time I connected on a body shot, it took a little more strength out of his legs. I knew if I could knock him down, he wouldn't be able to get up because his legs would be too weak.

In the tenth round, I landed a hard right to Moorer's forehead with such force that it made my hand hurt. I was surprised that he didn't go down. *What kind of man can take that sort of blow to the head and still remain standing?* But

I knew it wouldn't be long. He ducked when I threw a left hook, and then I remembered what I had seen in the dream. I followed up with a quick right-handed punch that knocked Moorer down to the canvas! As the referee started counting, I stepped back. I knew Michael wasn't going to get up.

I went to my corner, got on my knees, and prayed. If you see a picture of that knockdown, you won't find me standing over my opponent like I had done when I knocked Smokin' Joe Frazier to the canvas. Instead, you'll see me in my corner on my knees. I was sincerely thanking and praising God for this staggering victory.

Two records were broken that night. God had allowed me to become the oldest heavyweight boxing champion

> **GOD HAS A PLAN FOR EVERYONE, BUT AS YOU GET OLDER, YOUR ASSIGNMENTS MAY CHANGE.**

of all time at the age of forty-five. I also broke the record for a boxer with the most time in between one world championship and the next—twenty years.

But after winning the title, I didn't hang around to celebrate. Instead, I caught a flight that evening back to Houston and preached in my church the next morning. That was the best victory celebration I ever had!

YOU CAN START OVER

Just like I started over, you can too. God has a plan for everyone, but as you get older, your assignments may change. Maybe you're forty-seven years old and have been laid off from your job. Perhaps you've been a manager, a foreman, or a CEO but find yourself out of work because your company downsized. Or maybe you've lost your spouse through death or divorce. Now you have to start over.

Don't look at yourself as a has-been. The issue isn't your age. Nor does public opinion make much difference. It doesn't matter what people say about you because all things are possible with God. All that really matters is what God says about you and what you think and say about yourself. God can still use you to do great things. But you must first believe that the Lord wants to use you. You must say to yourself, *My best days are still ahead. I can do this.* Always see yourself as a person with a promising future.

Even if you've made a mess out of your life, it's not too late to change directions. If you've gone down the wrong road, you can still get back on the right path. God will lead you from where you are right now to where He wants you to be, if you'll let Him.

But be ready to start at the low end. You might think, *I've been at the top. Why should I have to go back to the bottom?* Because beginning at the bottom will give you a clearer perspective. You'll learn new and different ways to be successful. Starting over might even open up a completely different career for you. So congratulate yourself if you can see the bottom. The only way you can go is up. Hitting bottom might be the greatest thing that's ever happened to you!

Take your time. Don't rush it. When God told my wife I would be champion again, I didn't jump the gun just because I had already been champ. I knew it would take at least three to four years to get where I wanted to go, just like the first time—only tougher. We parents always tell our kids to be patient. But as we get older, patience seems to disappear from our own vocabularies. We, too, need to be patient, especially when it comes to reaching new goals.

If you want to be hired for a particular job, you may need to go back to trade school or college for three to four years. Why not? It's never too late to start doing what you love, even if it means starting all over again; you can discipline yourself to do it right. If you hope to establish a new relationship, you need to be rubbing shoulders with good, godly people around your age and with your interests. You can't simply sit home all the time, watching television and gorging yourself on junk food, while expecting God to send somebody wonderful into your life. Get involved in your church or community, serve others, and watch what God will do for you!

Dependency on God is an attitude that we must develop to be successful at any age. Moses was the humblest man on Earth, which meant he depended completely on the Lord. And that's why God was able to use him. Humility benefits us more than any athletic skill or intellectual capability. Dependency on God gives us a power that is greater than any human strength.

Some young athletes are so talented that it's easy for them to say, "God gave me my ability." They may say it, but do they really *believe* it? When an athlete scores a touchdown, he might point up to heaven as if the Lord had just done it. But when you truly grasp that God has given you the ability to succeed, you're so humbled that you're not interested in making a big show.

No matter how old you are, you can still start at the bottom and work your way up to the top. Have faith. Learn a new way. Depend on God. Take your time.

If I could do it, you can too.

ANOTHER COMEBACK?

In 1997, I retired from boxing with a record of 76 wins, 5 losses, and 69 knockouts. In 2003, I was inducted into the International Boxing Hall of Fame and named the ninth greatest puncher of all time by *Ring Magazine*.

I seriously considered another comeback at fifty-five years old, but my wife put a stop to that idea. I had started training and was losing weight. I told my wife,

HITTING BOTTOM MIGHT BE THE GREATEST THING THAT'S EVER HAPPENED TO YOU!

"Mary, I'm in better shape now than I've ever been in my life."

Mary looked back at me coolly. She said, "George, you're not going back to boxing."

At first, I thought she was joking, because Mary had never put any demands on me regarding my career.

"I'm sorry, but I'm going back," I said.

"Oh no you're not! I'm not going through *that* again. Last time you went back into boxing, we were broke and you needed to feed your family. That's why I went along with it then. But you've already won the title twice, so no more boxing!"

"But you believe that I can do it, don't you? I still have my strength, I've got my jab . . ."

"Isn't that the way you want to be remembered, George?"

"You can't tell me what to do," I said.

But she did. That was one fight that I had no chance of winning.

TIPS FROM GEORGE'S CORNER ON GROWING OLDER

- Realize that your life's experience gives you an advantage.
- Believe that God can still use you to accomplish His purposes.
- Adapt your abilities to utilize them to the fullest.
- Depend on God's strength and not your own.

17
WHY I NAMED ALL MY SONS GEORGE

PEOPLE OFTEN ASK ME WHY I NAMED ALL MY BOYS GEORGE. I always joke, "I fought Muhammad Ali, Joe Frazier, Ken Norton, and Evander Holyfield. You let those guys knock you in the head a few times, and see how many names you can remember!"

Actually, my real reason goes much deeper than that.

After I lost the championship title to Muhammad Ali in 1974, I returned to Houston to spend some time with my family. I felt totally dejected and worthless. Life didn't seem to matter anymore. Losing the title was bad enough, but my sister Gloria was about to drop another bombshell that would rock my world even more.

"I need to tell you something," she said. "Have you ever wondered why you don't look like the rest of us?"

"What are you talking about?"

"Daddy's not really your father."

"That's a lie!" I asserted.

"Remember when we used to call you 'Mo-head' when you were a kid? We were actually calling you Moorehead. That's your real father's name. I saw a letter he wrote to Momma. He wanted to meet you, but Mom wouldn't let him."

Again I denied it. "That's a lie!" I didn't want to hear Gloria's words, but I suspected that what she was saying might be true.

I called my dear Aunt Leola, my mother's sister, and made up a story to see if I could find out the truth. (Remember, this was before my spiritual conversion, so lying came all too easily to me.)

"Aunt Leola," I said as casually as I could, "I was training for a fight in Madison Square Garden when a man walked up to me and introduced himself. He said, 'Hey, George, I'm kin to you. I just wanted to tell you that I'm your daddy. My name is Leroy Moorehead.'" I paused for effect. I listened for a reaction and heard nothing but a deafening silence from Aunt Leola, so I continued.

"Now tell me the truth—was that man my father?"

"What?" Aunt Leola sounded shocked.

"Aunt Leola, I know you would never lie to me. Please tell me the truth. Is that man my father?"

Aunt Leola started sobbing. "Your mother would kill me. . . . "

She didn't have to say anything else. I knew Leroy Moorehead was my biological father. But I wanted to hear it from my mother because all my life, I had believed that J. D. Foreman was my real dad.

I called my mother and told her the same fabricated story. "Momma, I met a man at Madison Square Garden by the name of Leroy Moorehead. Do you know him? He says that he is my real father, not J.D. Foreman. Tell me the truth."

Immediately, my mother burst into tears. After composing herself, she said, "George, why do you think J. D. drinks?" She explained that J. D. and her had split up at that time, and that's when she met Leroy.

I was stunned. All my years, I had believed a lie—that J. D. Foreman was my father. Yet, J. D. was the only father I had known growing up. When I was a small boy, he would put his hand on my head and announce, "George Foreman, the next heavyweight champion of the world!" He loved me as his own child, and he never once hinted that he wasn't my real father.

After finding out the truth, I tracked down some information and arranged to meet Leroy Moorehead at a church in Marshall, Texas. He was a World War II veteran, a staff sergeant who had been wounded in battle in North Africa. He had followed my boxing career and bragged to his World War II buddies about being the father of the heavyweight champion.

"Yeah, right," his buddies said, laughing him off, of course.

But the man was telling them the truth.

Leroy Moorehead and I never really established a strong father-son bond, but at least we were able to talk and be close and have some semblance of a relationship for the rest of his life. When Leroy passed away in 1978, I conducted his funeral. As I stared at his body lying in the coffin, I thought, *That really was my father, and now he's passed on. This will never happen to my children. I will give them something they will never lose.*

So why did I name all my sons George Edward Foreman? Because I wanted to give them something in common, a sense of identity, so they would remember the family name. I told them, "When one George Edward Foreman does well, we all do well. But if one gets into trouble, our name goes down. So whatever you do now, you're not just doing it to yourself but to the entire family."

I tell them that if they ever get separated, all they need to do is look up their own name, and then they will find each other. My sons have a stronger bond among them because of their identical names. They really *love* one another. I've never seen a group of young men love each other so much. When the three older ones decide to go out to eat somewhere, they'll go get the two younger ones and take them along.

To keep everyone straight, we use nicknames. But sometimes those nicknames disappear and we just call each other "George." Although I have daughters, too, everyone wants to know about my sons because of their identical names. Here's a list of the Georges, from oldest to youngest:

George Edward Foreman Sr. That's me—"Big George."

George Edward Foreman Jr. is "Little George." He graduated from Wiley College in Marshall, Texas, and received his master's degree from

LSU. He has worked for the district attorney in Marshall and currently works for Wiley College as the director of Alumni Relations.

George Edward Foreman III is "Monk." He is my business manager, having attended Pepperdine University in California and graduated from Rice University in Houston. He plans to get his master's degree at Rice.

George Edward Foreman IV is "Big Wheel." He recently graduated from high school and plays football at the University of Redlands in California. He has done so many things well and is always quick to say, "Thank You, Jesus."

George Edward Foreman V is "Red." We call him Red because he was supposed to be the "stop sign." He attends high school, where he enjoys all sports but loves basketball the most.

George Edward Foreman VI is "Joe," named after my wife's father. He's strong and independent, even at seven years old.

Besides all those fine, handsome boys, I have five beautiful daughters. I came close to naming them all George, too, but I thought that might be over-doing things a bit. Instead, we named them Michi, Freeda George (I really came close with her name, didn't I?), Georgetta (almost!), Natalie, and Leola.

My daughters span the spectrum as far as their personalities, abilities, and aspirations, but each one is convinced she wants to succeed on her own merits, in her own arena, not simply on the basis of being my offspring. Michi, for example, is a talented singer, an artist with the soul of a poet, I like to say, and the quick wit of a stand-up comedian. Natalie, a graduate of Baylor University, is currently furthering her education. She is a bright, determined young woman who will probably be one of the world's great doctors. Georgetta, who graduated from Pepperdine University, loves to write and is the most serious of my daughters; she loves to contemplate dif-ficult issues and present her own independent perspectives on them. Leola is our youngest daughter and is named after my favorite aunt. She exudes a special "class" and commands respect even from people who meet her for the first time. Outgoing and confident, Leola has never met an enemy; she could make a friend of almost anyone.

Maybe it is not surprising that the child I had the most problems with was the daughter I named George. The third of my ten children, Freeda George and I had a strained relationship at various points throughout her late teen years. She once even brought false charges against me that nearly ripped my heart out. Just as we finally got our relationship on track and were enjoying better days, Freeda announced that she planned to become a boxer!

Women's boxing was growing as a sport, and Laila Ali and Jacqui Frazier-Lyde, daughters of Muhammad Ali and Joe Frazier, respectively, had already achieved some measure of success as boxers. Freeda figured she could do the same or better.

As a little girl, Freeda fought against an even more formidable foe: food. Thanks to her mother and me, she learned early on that french fries, hamburgers, pizza, ice cream, and other treats could make the best day even better. We were delighted that Freeda had such a strong appetite. Although she played sports in school, her growing weight problem caused her friends to shy away, and she began spending more and more time at home, in front of a television, snacking.

We did everything we knew to help her—sending her to counseling, weight loss centers, nutritionists, and more. Nothing seemed to help. When she took up boxing, however, she started exercising and jogging several miles every day, and the weight began to fall off her body. By the time she was twenty-three, when she was scheduled for her first bout in Las Vegas, she was in tip-top shape.

Nevertheless, I adamantly opposed my daughter's following my footsteps into the boxing ring. She was so pretty; I couldn't stand the thought of my baby being punched. I tried my best to convince her not to go into boxing, even avoiding her for a while, but she was insistent.

"Daddy, this is something I've always wanted to do," she said. I had playfully sparred with all my girls as they grew up, so boxing was not unfamiliar to them. But this was different. Freeda was stepping into the ring with another woman who wanted to knock her out!

I refused to attend the fight, hoping that my absence might deter Freeda. I thought, *Maybe if she realizes how strongly I oppose her boxing, she might reconsider.* But to Freeda, boxing was about her self-esteem and sense of accomplishment. She ignored my concerns and stepped into the ring.

She wasn't there long. By 1:44 of the second round, Freeda had floored her opponent, LaQuanda Landers, and had won a technical knockout. It was Father's Day. After the fight, surrounded by the media, Freeda said, "Happy Father's Day, Daddy. This is for you. I love you."

Freeda won several more fights, and she started attending church with the other members of our family after each match that she won. It was a real conundrum for me: there was my daughter doing what I didn't want her to do—boxing—but she was also doing what I wanted her to do the most—getting into church and developing a closer relationship with God.

I decided that for the time being, I had to relate to my daughter differently—I saw her as my daughter, but I also saw her as a child of God coming through the church doors. I devoted lots of time to Freeda, not simply as my daughter, but as a young woman searching for the peace of God in her heart. One of the greatest joys of my life was to hear my daughter say to me one day, "Dad, I am ready to be baptized." I had waited years to hear those words coming from Freeda's mouth, and I knew she would never make that statement until she had wholeheartedly decided to live for God.

I attended Freeda's last boxing match—one that I promoted—in Houston. She lost the bout, but she won a lot of new fans, including me. I was so impressed with Freeda; there was no "quit" in her, no giving up, even in the losing effort.

Freeda retired from boxing and started working as the executive director at the George Foreman Youth and Community Center. She visits schools, speaking to young people about developing good diet and exercise habits; she also emphasizes the importance of finding and hanging out with the right kinds of friends and, of course, developing a friendship with God. She began hosting boxing matches at the center and even promoted a number of amateur fights in Texas, including "Houston's Night of Stars." Freeda has become my right-hand person at the youth center, and she now uses the name Freeda George Foreman with pride.

But I need to tell you about one more George—George Edward—the one you read about in the first chapter. You're probably wondering what ever happened to the boy I prayed for to be healed—my nephew, George Edward Dumas. He's now six feet six inches and weighs more than two hundred fifty pounds. He also works for me, training my horses and, of course, serving as my security guard!

TIPS FROM GEORGE'S CORNER
ON LEAVING A LEGACY

- Make sure that you're living in a way that your children will be honored by your name.
- Although your children are all different, treat them equally with love.

18
WILL I MEET YOU IN HEAVEN?

AFTER CHURCH ONE DAY, MY COUSIN HENRY ROBERTS INTRODUCED me to Richard Johnson, a young man who had come along with him to the service. Mr. Johnson told me, "I was visiting at one of your homes years ago with Henry, when I was just a young boy. We spent the day swimming in your pool, and Henry gave us some food to eat, too. But I never got a chance to meet you till today."

That's the way it is for a lot of people when it comes to having a relationship with the good Lord. They live on God's earth, eat His food, and enjoy His blessings; they know a lot about Him, but they've never really met Him.

Mr. Johnson, I soon learned, shared a passion to help other people. He was a good man who had been involved in politics and had worked with young people as well, helping them to get a better start in life. Then life took its toll on him, and he suffered some severe setbacks. That's part of what brought him to the church. He started attending our services on a regular basis, and it was plain to see that he was looking for some hope. One day, when I talked to him at church, I could smell the alcohol on his breath. I didn't say anything to him about his drinking, but not long after that, I was speaking on the subject of not causing someone else to stumble.

I wasn't really thinking about Mr. Johnson in particular, but I said, "What about all the people who look up to you? Imagine if I decided to take a drink when I was out someplace by myself. I could rationalize it and say, 'No one will ever know,' but God sees everything. He knows. So we should live as though we are putting on a show for God."

Apparently God used those words to touch Mr. Johnson's heart and mind. After hearing that message, Mr. Johnson decided to turn his life around. It wasn't easy for him, but he stayed with the process and God helped him to get his life back on track. He later said, "I was always trying to find that same joy that George had. How could he endure what he had and still keep a smile on his face? Whatever it was, I wanted it."

Not only did Mr. Johnson find that joy for himself; he's been able to help a lot of other people find it as well. Eventually, he became a preacher and a good one, too! Pastor Richard Johnson has been responsible for building a number of churches in Louisiana and also has an extremely effective ministry to inmates in prisons.

That's what my life is all about these days—helping one person help another. I love pointing people toward heaven, sharing with them God's plan of salvation in such a simple way that even a child can understand it. I want people to know that they matter to God, that He hasn't given up on them, that He is interested in every detail of their lives. That's a message that is close to my heart.

One time I was lying in bed at my home in Marshall, Texas, when a "man" appeared to me. He was dressed in a fine white robe, but I couldn't make out his face. He spoke kindly to me: "Brother George, my Father is concerned about you." He didn't identify himself, but I think I know who it was who spoke those words to me that night.

And the message is the same for you: Your heavenly Father is concerned about you; He loves you and wants to have a close relationship with you. God is in your corner.

My brother, Roy Foreman, needed to be reminded of that message as well. Roy was running low on faith and was nearly depleted of hope after I retired from boxing, and our lives took different turns. Roy knew as well as anybody that the transformation of my life was real; he had been in that dressing room in Puerto Rico the night I found God. But he never accepted it. He never experienced it for himself.

Years later, when I visited Roy at the gym where he was working with kids, teaching them to box, I told my brother, "There's a step higher, Roy. And you can take it."

"George, I think I want that. I want to find true peace."

"Then give God a chance, Roy."

My brother started attending church with me for the first time. He said he wanted to find the peace that I talked about. One day as I was preaching, Roy saw something that made him think. As I was speaking about how God had promised to help the Israelites, assuring them that even small numbers of them would put the enemy to flight and that their land would always produce crops, Roy took that message to heart. He began trusting God and serving in church. He became a better husband and father and to this day thanks me for helping him to be a better man. That's what having God in your corner can do for a person.

It's simple really. If I offered to give you a hundred-dollar bill, I could hold it out to you, but it doesn't become yours until you reach out and take it. God's gift of salvation is received in much the same way. But instead of taking it with your hand, you receive it with your heart.

That's what my good friend, Michael Harris, did. When Michael first visited our church, he had just about given up on God and had definitely given up on his marriage. A brilliant man and a popular radio show host in Houston, Michael told me, "I have never said this to you before, but, George, you seem to have a peace that I've always wanted."

"You can have it, too, Michael," I told him. "What God has done for me, He can do for you, but you gotta fight for it. You have to want it. Same with your marriage. I know God can heal your marriage, but you have to want Him to do it, and you have to be willing to fight to save what is good and let go of anything that is bad."

Each time I saw Michael at church or in social circles, I encouraged him to trust God and reminded him of his great love that he had for his wife. Sometimes Michael looked at me as though I was talking about someone else, but I wasn't. I was envisioning by faith his life being transformed by God.

Then Michael's wife became deathly sick and, suddenly, this couple that was on the verge of losing it all asked God to save not just her life but also their marriage. Today, seeing Michael and his wife together is like seeing one person. They are so much in love and Michael's peace is so great. Not long ago, Michael Harris preached a sermon at our church, and his wife sat there beaming with pride at the man, the preacher, and the loving husband she knew. God can still work miracles when we trust Him.

If you want to know more about God's plan for your life, start reading the Bible, just as I did. The Gospel of John is a good place to begin. And talk to God every day. Tell Him about all of the good things and the difficult circumstances you are facing. He already knows, but like a good earthly father, your heavenly Father is interested in everything about your life, including what you are feeling.

It's also important that you find a good church that teaches and preaches about Jesus. Make sure the people of that congregation love the good Lord, and then you can become a part of that fellowship. Live for God every day, knowing that your life is in His hands. He's the best trainer of all, and He will prepare you and guide you through every challenge of life. And His retirement plan is "out of this world"!

When our lives on Earth are over, we'll go to be with the Lord forever to live in our eternal home. Now, I've lived in some beautiful homes during my lifetime, but from what I've read in the Bible, if we think we've had some mansions here on Earth, we haven't seen anything yet! Just wait till you get a glimpse of the place that Jesus has been preparing for you.

I hope to meet you in heaven someday. I'm going to be there, and I hope you'll join me in the eternal celebration. In the meantime, if anybody asks you why you are so happy, you can tell them the same thing I do: "I have God in my corner."

TIPS FROM GEORGE'S CORNER
ON LIVING AS A CHRISTIAN

- Read a chapter from the Bible every morning.
- Talk to the Lord throughout the day, letting Him know everything that's on your heart.
- Get involved in a church that believes the entire Bible, and where the members are joyful.

ACKNOWLEDGMENTS

SPECIAL THANKS TO MY SON, GEORGE III, "MONK", FOR ALL HIS hard work on this project. This book could not have been done without him.

Thanks to my friend and literary agent Henry Holmes—friends to the end.

I am also deeply grateful to Doc Broadus. Thank God he saw in me that special something that made him willing to work with me. He helped me become a champion in and out of the ring.

To Joe Frazier, one of the greatest heavyweight champions of the world.

And special thanks to my Leola, whom I hope to meet again in heaven one day.

Also thanks to Greg Daniel and the great sales team of Thomas Nelson Publishers for believing in this book, and to Thom Chittom, our editor, who helped keep us on track.

Thanks also to Mark Sweeney who represented Ken Abraham on this project, and to Kent Crockett, Ken's assistant, who was a tremendous help.

NOTES

CHAPTER 2—THE DAY I DIED
1. See Acts 9:1–18.

CHAPTER 3—GET ME A HIT MAN
1. See Matthew 18:22–35.

CHAPTER 4—WHAT WILL PEOPLE THINK OF ME?
1. See Acts 10:1–4.

CHAPTER 5—A FIGHTING PREACHER
1. Colossians 3:1.

CHAPTER 6—BEING OPTIMISTIC IN A PESSIMISTIC WORLD
1. Luke 23:34.

CHAPTER 7—APPRECIATE TODAY
1. Psalm 23:6.
2. Matthew 6:11.

CHAPTER 8—GOD WILL DIRECT YOUR STEPS
1. "His Eye Is on the Sparrow," Civilla D. Martin, 1905.
2. Psalm 1:1.
3. Proverbs 3:5–6.

CHAPTER 9—THE WORST THING CAN BE THE BEST THING
1. Romans 8:28.
2. See Genesis 39:2–3, 21, 23.
3. See Genesis 50:20.

CHAPTER 10—INSPIRING OTHERS TO EXCELLENCE

1. ContraCostaTimes.com, June 4, 2006, http://www.contracostatimes.com/mld/cctimes/news/local/states/california/14739108.htm.
2. Philippians 2:3 NASB.

CHAPTER 11—ADVANCING THROUGH ADVERSITY

1. Job 1:21.
2. Job 13:15.

CHAPTER 12—INTEGRITY—DON'T LEAVE HOME WITHOUT IT

1. Genesis 4:7.
2. Job 31:1.
3. Psalm 84:11.
4. Proverbs 20:7.

CHAPTER 14—THE SECRET OF SUCCESS

1. Matthew 6:33.
2. Psalm 1:1-3.

CHAPTER 15—DO YOUR GIVING WHILE YOU'RE LIVING

1. Acts 20:35.
2. Psalm 37:25.
3. Luke 6:38–9 NASB.
4. Matthew 6:20.

CHAPTER 16—AGE FORTY ISN'T A DEATH SENTENCE

1. Matthew 5:5.

ABOUT THE AUTHORS

GEORGE FOREMAN, once boxing's heavyweight champion of the world, is best known today as an entrepreneur and philanthropist. He is a frequent speaker at nationwide events. George is an ordained minister and preaches twice a week in his church in Houston. He is the father of ten.

KEN ABRAHAM is a *New York Times* best-selling author known around the world for his collaborations with high-profile public figures. His recent books include *Against All Odds* with Chuck Norris, and *Let's Roll!* with Lisa Beamer, widow of United Flight 93 hero Todd Beamer.

CPSIA information can be obtained
at www.ICGtesting.com
Printed in the USA
BVHW032115170423
662535BV00002B/6

9 781400 339853